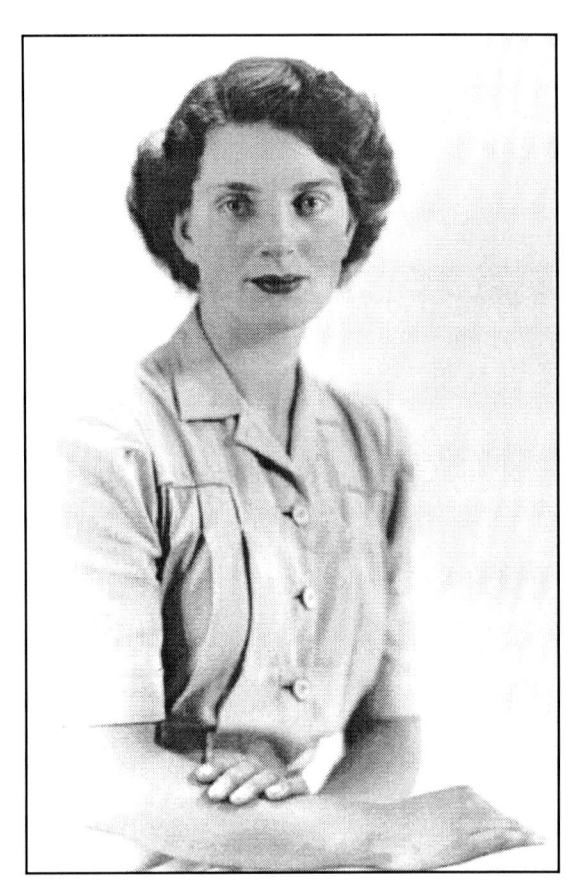

RUTH HARVEY

PAINTINGS & COLLAGES

4

RUTH   HARVEY

PAINTINGS   &   COLLAGES

by

Elizabeth   Haines

and

David   Harvey,
Editor.

HELIOTROPE   PUBLISHING

6

First published privately in 1995,
as a limited edition of 500 copies
of which this is number   .

. . . .

British Library
Cataloguing-in-Publication Data.

A catalogue record for this book is
available from the British Library.

ISBN   0 9523431 1 8

Printed and published by
Heliotrope Publishing,   c/o
The Slough, Jameston, near Tenby,
Pembrokeshire, Wales, SA70 7SR .

Set principally in Garamond 12 on 14 pt.

Contents

*   *   *   *   *   *   *

List of Plates

Plates continued ...

See Editor's note opposite concerning the 'unknown' pictures.
Picture sizes exclude the frames, and are in inches 'Height by Width'.
The Frontispiece photograph shows Ruth in her early twenties.

AUTHOR'S NOTE.

I have generally used the words 'he' and 'his' throughout the text, even though they are clearly meant to include both men and women artists. The alternative s/he is unobtrusive but the constant repetition of his/her less so, and I felt that whatever might be gained was outweighed by the unwieldiness involved. I apologise to any ardent feminists who take exception to this.

Elizabeth Haines, 1995.

EDITOR'S NOTE.

It is not our intention to repeat much of the biographical data to be found in Vol I ; likewise only a few pictures have been repeated - where it is important to illustrate a point being made. The publisher will be delighted to assist anyone lacking Volume I, and I can confirm that Vol III is planned in 1996, focusing mainly on 'Pembrokeshire'.

Some important pictures are only available to us via Ruth's own photographs taken many years ago. The quality of these (Instamatic) photos is not ideal and they have generally been reproduced at half-size to maintain reasonable definition; also I have had to guess at the titles ! The owners of these pictures are unknown to me at the time of writing and I must trespass upon their goodwill in publishing without notice or proper acknowledgement. However, I am advised that the copyright does actually still reside with the artist and her estate.

I am always happy to hear from owners of Ruth's pictures, and particularly those mentioned above, of course, in case we can do better justice to them in a later volume or edition.

David Harvey, 1995.

Preface

"All things counter, original, spare, strange;"
'Pied Beauty', Gerard Manley Hopkins.

Whatever Ruth Harvey's religious beliefs, her work is a song of praise - praise for those choice things and places she selected from the humdrum, and for those even more rare and special qualities they could reveal to her penetrating artist's eye.

This book presents a wide selection of her drawings, paintings and collages, showing us something of their physical substance and qualities of expressiveness, colour, design, etc ... , while Elizabeth Haines' illuminating text provides a rationale for them of which the artist herself was clearly considerably aware. We must welcome her son David's initiative in arranging this book, for Ruth's work deserves to be better known.

She seldom exhibited except in the homely setting of a corridor and studio - which together served as a gallery in her house. Indeed, she seems to have been content to *do* rather than to show or sell more widely. Perhaps this favoured the unhurried concentration on the working out of each piece in the privacy of her own artistic voyage, a concentration and attention to detail which underlies much of her work.

She also showed great courage in pressing on against increasing disability and all difficulties, including the loss of Michael - her husband and constant support - and continued a steady though diminishing output to within a year of her death.

Despite the sharp variations of approach and treatment, a browse through the illustrations should give an overall impression of certain predominant qualities that almost invariably shine through, irrespective of the artist's present preoccupation in any particular piece of work. These are the essential qualities of the artist.

Her work is modest and experimental - and therein lies its genuineness and its strength. She does not elaborate, flourish or toy with design or colour, rather putting things down and leaving them - an enviable ability which gives a spareness, almost astringency to much of her work.

Simplicity and clarity of statement seem to come very naturally to her, but her certainty of line and tone may also evolve as she works through several versions of the same subject - from drawing to watercolour to collage, as in the 'Drive to Blackawton' series. Each medium contributes a different experience of the subject as the artist's perception of it becomes more selective and satisfying. Such developments evidently led her towards collage - the medium in which she found the greatest release.

In collage, Ruth's breezy open landscape style achieves a grandeur of spaciousness. Intricately cut papers 'draw' the landscape as a series of sweeping linear and tonal harmonies, her choice range of patterned and textured papers fulfilling a strong *expressive* purpose with no concessions to the perhaps more commonplace *decorative* use of collage.

The span of Ruth's work can also be illustrated by her range of Still Life pictures (only a few of these are shown here, of which plate 31 'Cherries' is the best example), where a cluster of jewel-like small fruit nestle in a small dish, a glass bowl or a basket standing on a faintly shadowed surface. Nothing more. Here is a rare purity and simplicity, poles away from her roistering landscapes or angulated buildings.

Boats & buildings, a wasp jar, an old petrol pump, a beautifully fashioned copper propeller, a buoy or a bollard .... any object surprising or characterful in colour or shape (particularly in shape) intrigued her mind and eye, and led her on. Her pleasure in these 'ordinary' things made them worthy of her notice and response.

Many of her works can be seen as more complex responses to "things counter, original, spare, strange" or to more elaborate examples of them. A thin iron railing rears, curving against a grey sky, delicately setting off the shapes of greys and whites of a marine building on 'The Cob at Lyme Regis' (plate 2). This oil might be anyone's first choice, but readers will find their own favourites and, in the light of Elizabeth Haines' highly pertinent text, appreciate many others more fully.

If the publication of Ruth Harvey's work in this form attracts the interest it deserves, perhaps we may hope that a worthy exhibition may also follow.

Wendy Gillett.
November 1995.

INTRODUCTION

INTRODUCTION

"I am a part of all that I have met" declared Ulysses in Tennyson's poem of that name. As well as being part of it, all that we have met, experienced and read about also becomes gradually, imperceptibly, a part of us. This is demonstrably true of the artist, writer or composer, and in their works we are able to trace certain influences which they absorb and assimilate into their own personal expression.

In the same way we can recognise in the child features from the parents. Expressions, gestures and attitudes are both inherited and consciously copied; they may manifest themselves only fleetingly, or constitute a fundamental part of the self [1].

We may also consciously reject attitudes and ideas from our parents, but they are inescapably a part of our inheritance. We measure ourselves against them and also against our contemporaries, particularly during the developmental period of childhood and youth. In all the arts the tradition of one's predecessors, especially the 'parent' generation, is similarly vital, as are the activities of those who work alongside us.

---

1. I was reminded of Ruth's poem 'Heredity' (see Appendix), in which she asks ..... " .... Of what account
That strange elusive likeness to one's kin ?"

This elusive likeness is also discernible amongst groups of artists whose reciprocal influence upon each others' work gives a certain family feeling, particularly if they are viewed together. This coherence, which transcends differences in personality, is attributable to shared ideals and is evident in, for example, the work of the Bloomsbury Group - Roger Fry, Duncan Grant, Vanessa Bell and others.

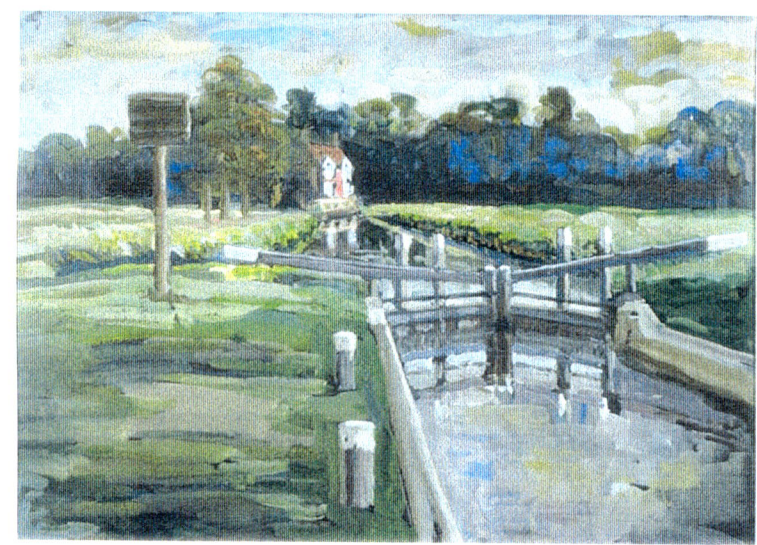

Plate 1.   Unstead Lock, Surrey (Gouache) H x W 12 x 17.
Plate 2.   The Cob, Lyme Regis, looking west (Oil) 16 x 20.

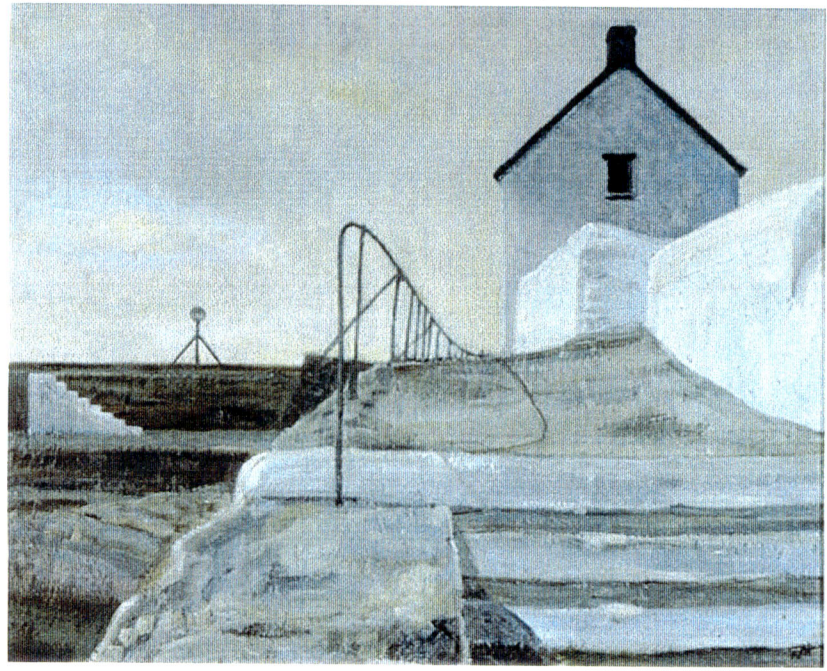

Today, by virtue of the advances in technology, our perception of the work of other artists is by no means limited to those of our own area. By contrast, two hundred years ago any artist had to undertake often long and arduous journeys to study the works of others. Dürer, for example, visited Italy twice from Germany, and his contact with Italian painters profoundly affected not only his way of working but his high conception of the artist's role.

Bach did not venture so far afield, but as a young man he walked from Lüneburg to Hamburg to hear Reinken play the organ at St Katherine's church, and some years later made his way, again on foot, some 200 miles from Arnstadt to Lübeck to hear Buxtehüde.

Nowadays it could be said that we suffer from a surfeit or 'anxiety' of influences. A performance of a new musical work can be heard simultaneously in many countries, and film or photographs of a new exhibition are available almost as quickly, followed by (often contradictory) reviews as to the work's merit.

In this situation an artist often has a harder task to establish his own identity than in the past, when he would find himself as part of a much more clearly defined tradition; often working in the master's studio for several years and only when he had assimilated that particular style would he be in a position to develop his own interests and ideas.

On the other hand, the artist may find his niche more quickly by being exposed nowadays to such a wide range of influences, instead of one main school, and indeed the discipline of the old master's apprenticeship might sometimes even have had a dampening effect on the pupil's creativity.

Ruth certainly experimented widely with both materials and styles, and it is to her credit that she was able to do so with such competence. We in turn now reap the benefit of seeing the full range of this work.

As to the issue of identity we will explore this further, but it has not proved difficult to uncover the recurring ideas which prompted her, however diverse the presentation.

The foregoing serves to establish a context for the theme of this book about Ruth Harvey, where I will trace some of the interests which were a formative influence upon her own work. These influences will be considered in context of Ruth's various spheres of special interest - landscape & buildings, still life, water, music, and industrial & maritime artefacts.

Within the general category of landscapes comes a special preoccupation with pathways, gates and alternative 'ways to go'. Water in all its forms was a fascination - Locks, canals, waveforms, the ebb & flow of tidal water, and snow.

Ruth appears to have shown a greater propensity for music rather than the visual arts in her early years [2], and although there seem to be no actual drawings or paintings surviving from that period, she must have absorbed something of her father's interest in painting, and undoubtedly inherited his aptitude.

The outbreak of war in 1939 meant that she was involved in the war effort rather than pursuing a formal education in the arts, and subsequently the life of a naval officer's wife meant frequent moves. However, her interest in the visual arts was sufficiently strong for her to take the steps of enrolling successively at Portsmouth College of Art, Dartington, and the Camden Arts Centre.

Ruth hardly ever dated her work, which makes a chronological appraisal somewhat difficult. The many books and catalogues she acquired, however, enable us to fix some of the general periods of 'incoming information', and we also know that she did not start making collages until, perhaps, 1970 or later.

It seems that the years 1965-68, when her husband Michael was posted to the Ministry of Defence in London, were a vital period. Ruth clearly took full advantage of the many exhibitions on offer, as she had done previously in 1962-3 when the family lived briefly in St. John's Wood.

Ruth also bought several notable prints and original paintings which reflected not only her interest in maritime subjects, but also a keen awareness of contemporary art forms.

2.   See 'Ruth Harvey - Art & Poetry', David Harvey, Heliotrope Publishing, 1994, p19.

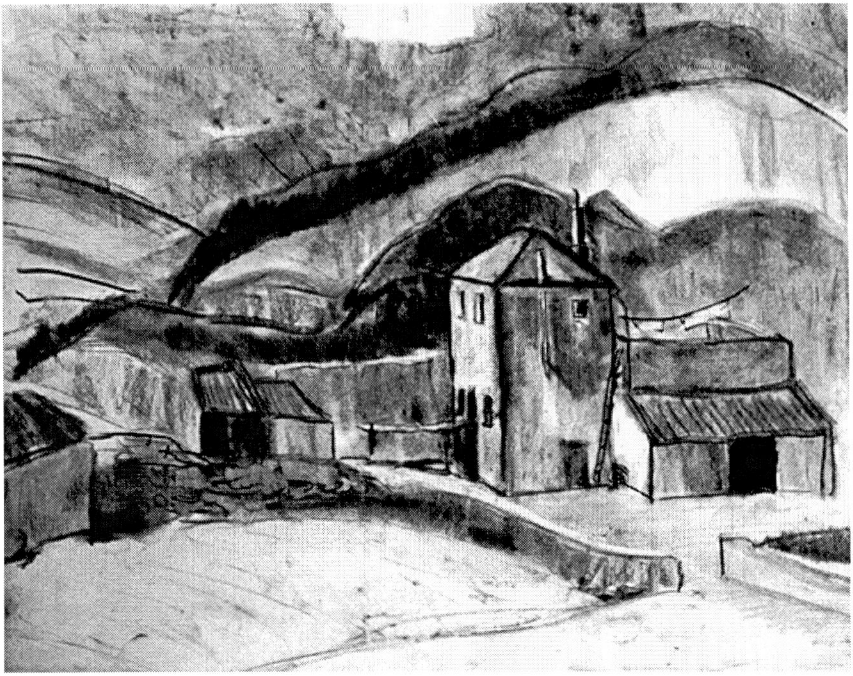

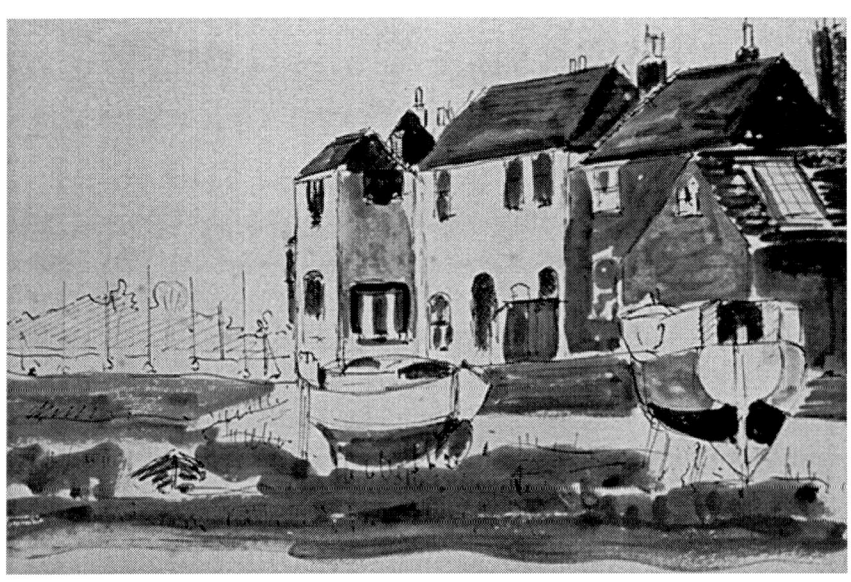

Plate 3.   Farmhouse   (Chalk drawing)   14 x 19.

Plate 4,   Bosham, Hants (Pencil & wash) 7 x 11.

Plate 5,   Holed Stone, Men-an-Tol, Cornwall,
        (Chalk drawing)   15 x 16.

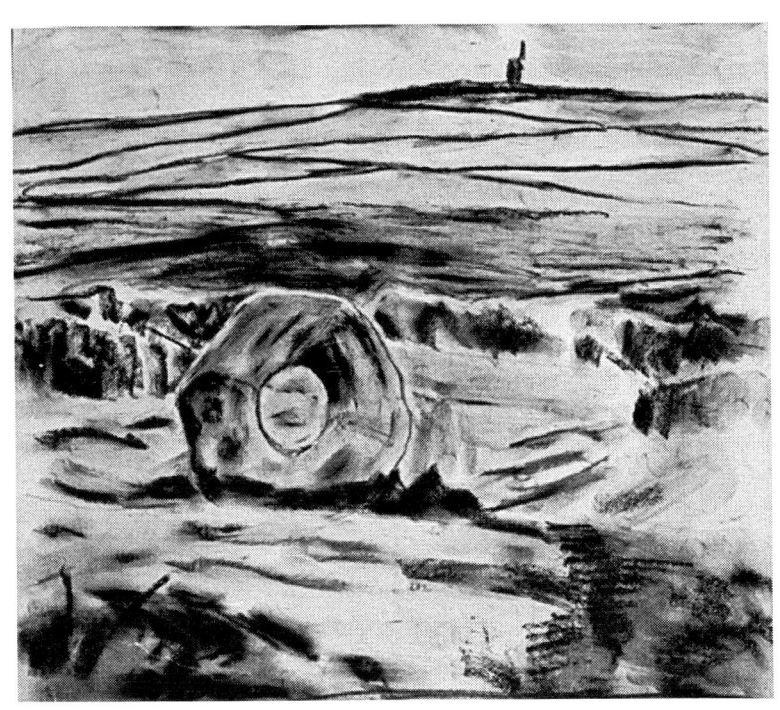

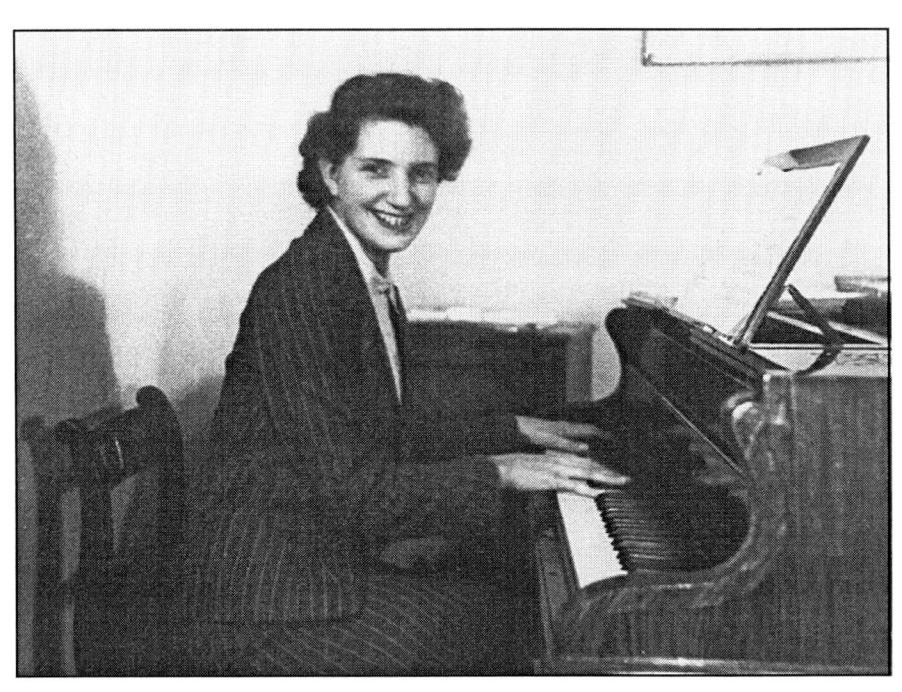

Ruth, aged about 20.

Her work prior to this period seems to be comprised mostly of bold landscape studies together with the exterior architecture of buildings (e.g. plates 1-6). It would seem that during this time she also ventured into abstraction, with compositions based on her studies from life, having been stimulated by works she saw in galleries or books.

Her keen interest in all the arts is evident from the many newspaper cuttings she collected, and poems which she copied out for her own reference; the particular patterns of interest which emerge from these will be studied in the Conclusion. Although few of these cuttings are dated, we are able to identify an ongoing preoccupation with certain themes which to some extent relate to the subjects of her pictures.

Before considering these influences, we may try to identify Ruth's individual strengths and weaknesses, and then see how she capitalised on them. She possessed a natural sense of colour harmony, as her early works show. Her early perspective drawing is sometimes shaky, but an equal ability in both spheres is unusual. The natural draughtsman may not have an intuitive feel for colour and composition, and vice versa with the painter.

William Blake explores this dichotomy in his interesting comparison 'Who is line : who is colour' [3], and numerous other writings on the subject suggest that our ability to perceive and handle colour is a 'right-brain' function, more intuitive

3.   See 'William Blake's Theory of Art', Morris Eaves,
      Princetown University Press, 1982, p18.

than logical, while the act of drawing is more aligned to the intellectual or 'left-brain'. As Michael Ayrton commented, the artist "....... draws to give order to his thought, whereas he may paint to give ease to his heart" [4].

Some examples from Ruth's portfolio, which presumably were not considered good enough for framing, show this natural grasp of colour relationships. 'Tin Bath' (gouache on black paper, plate 7) employs a muted but beautifully 'in tune' range of earth red, white, blue and green.

'Boat-house' (plate 8) also has simple areas of colour laid on 'alla prima' (no retouching) with a lovely chord created between the red facade and the green door. Simplicity of shapes on the picture plane is of prime importance here. Above all, these studies show a direct grasp of the subjects, and our enjoyment of them in turn directs us to a new awareness of the subject itself.

Ruth was painstaking in her approach and would spend hours absorbed in attaining exactly what she knew she wanted for a particular composition. This perfectionism persisted throughout her artistic life despite increasingly severe arthritis which took its toll generally, and did not spare her wrists and fingers. You would not think so from the clarity of the results - you have only to look at the collages which she produced in her last few years for evidence of this.

4.   See 'The Rudiments of Paradise', Michael Ayrton,
      Secker & Warburg, 1971, p170.

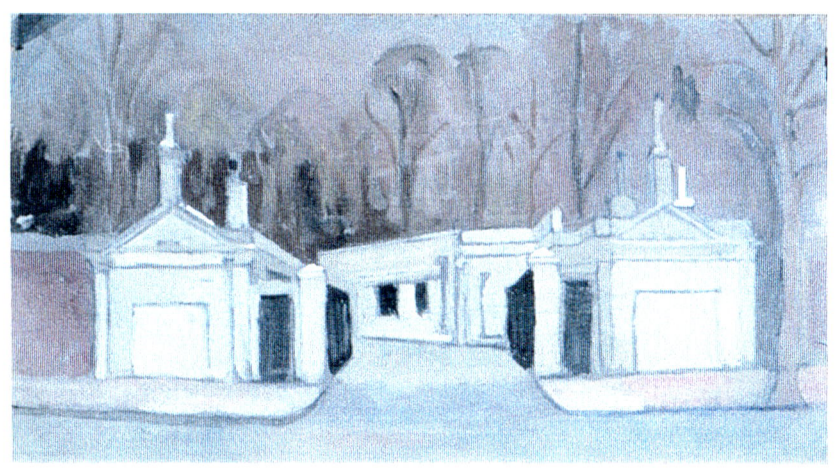

Plate 6. Lodge buildings (Gouache on blue paper) 10 x 19.
Plate 7. Tin Bath (Gouache on black paper) 16 x 10.
Plate 8. Boat-house (Gouache, normal paper) 13 x 8.

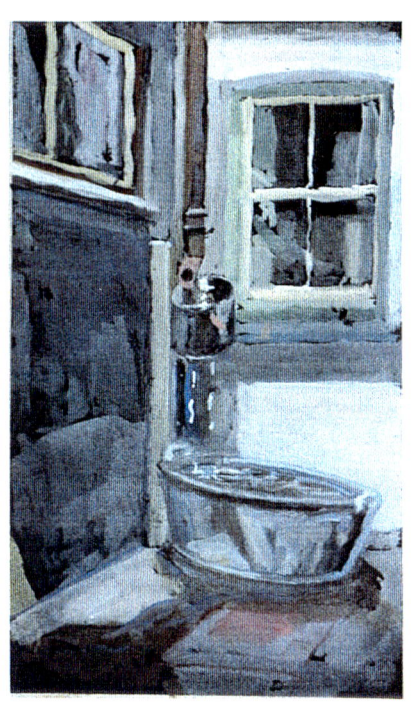

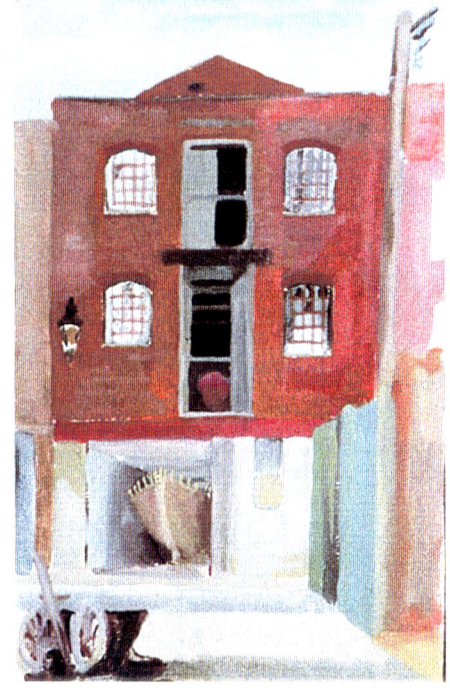

PART ONE

Chapter 1.

BASIC DESIGN.

Undoubtedly the periods at Portsmouth College of Art, Dartington Hall and Camden Art Centre had their influence on Ruth. The very fact that she embarked on this study of her own volition implies willingness to learn and absorb new ideas.

Amongst her papers are a number of 'Basic Design' studies which appear to have been done at one or other of these centres. Basic Design was much in vogue in Foundation courses during the 1960's, and its precepts were largely those of the Bauhaus at Weimar.

Between the founding of the Bauhaus in 1919 and its closure in 1933, a whole pedagogic system of design was built up on certain principles, and its effects were far reaching. The basic course at the Bauhaus required three areas of study.

Firstly, the analytical study of the raw materials of painting, sculpture and the crafts, to learn at first hand their expressive potential.   Secondly, free 'abstract' composition, which involved exploring the purely formal relationships between shape and colour, and the qualities of rhythm, balance and proportion which underlie even the most figurative works of visual art.   Thirdly, the analysis of existing works of art in terms of these structural qualities was also important.

The demise of the Bauhaus in the face of Nazi repression did not, however, destroy either their ideology or methodology - Gropius, Itten, Klee and Kandinsky, the major Bauhaus teachers, left an extensive legacy of published material [1].

Writers such as Roger Fry were grappling with similar themes - as were the De Stijl painters in Holland - and the influence of 'Formalism' can be seen in British painters such as Ben Nicholson.

During the 1960's Ruth was able to relate the experience of these studies to works which she enjoyed at first hand in her frequent visits to the London Galleries.

If we examine the art school exercise 'Colour Contrasts' (pl 9) and compare it with one of Ben Nicholson's more severe abstracts - his 'Painting' 1939 or 'Project for Painted Relief' 1943 spring to mind (these can be found in many books on this artist) - we can see in these elegant finished works the raison d'etre of this kind of study. Stripped of all 'content' - such as representation of, or allusion to, objects or scenes - the shapes and colours are allowed to interact in our mind's eye without the distractions of a 'storyline'.

1.   For example .....
      'The Art of Colour', J. Itten, Van Nostrand Reinhold, 1973.
      'On Modern Art', P. Klee, Faber & Faber, 1948.
      'Concerning the Spiritual in Art', W. Kandinsky,
          Translated by M.T.H. Sadler, Dover Books, 1977.

If we then look at the collage on plate 10, even though dating from as late as 1981, the amalgam of these influences is quite clear. The careful placing of the shapes, the constrained colour harmony and the imaginative use of material (the shapes are constructed from cut sandpapers) all bear witness to her having assimilated the purpose of the exercises. Also, Ruth, perhaps not feeling absolutely happy with pure abstraction, suggests a minimal storyline with her title 'Sun and Moon'.

A number of her books contain reproductions of Nicholson's works, as do catalogues from various London art galleries. Even when not in London and away from the mainstream of contemporary art she nevertheless, unobtrusively and with quiet determination, assembled a collection of material which would nourish her own ideas and extend her vision.

Ruth produced very few such severe works as 'Sun and Moon'. Perhaps the decision not to pursue formalism as an end in itself meant that her real interest lay in using what she had learned to reappraise her experience of the world as she saw it.

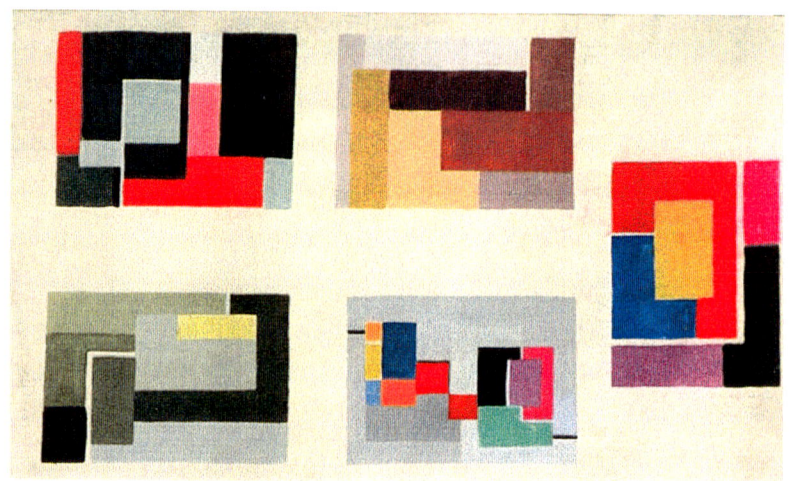

Plate 9.   Colour contrasts (Gouache) 12 x 20.

Plate 10.   Sun and Moon (Collage, sandpapers) 10 x 13.
Courtesy of Mr & Mrs N. Bateman.

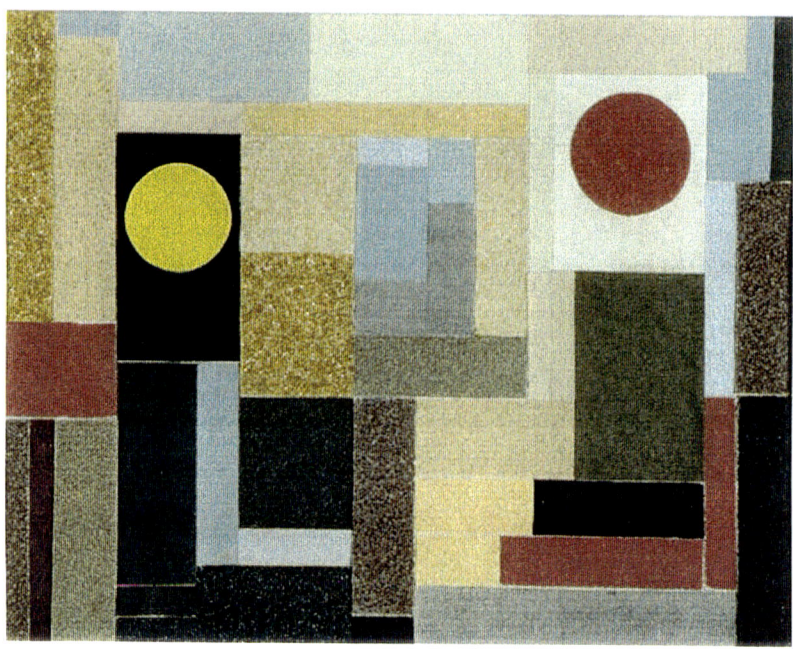

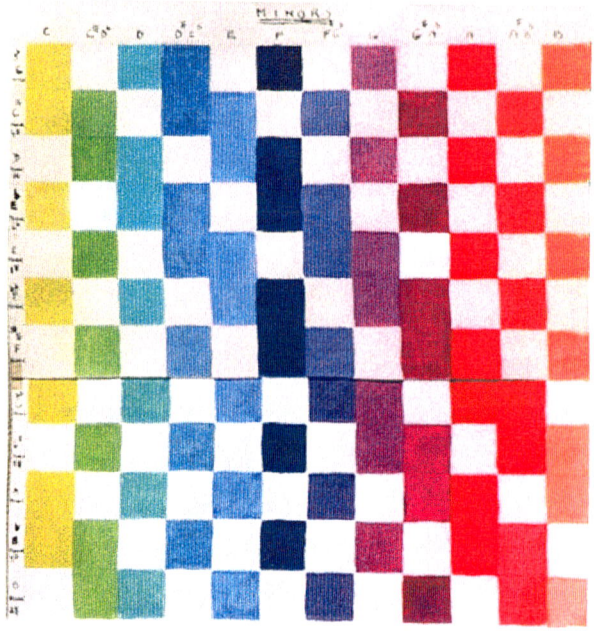

Plate 11.
Minors
(Gouache)
14 x 12.

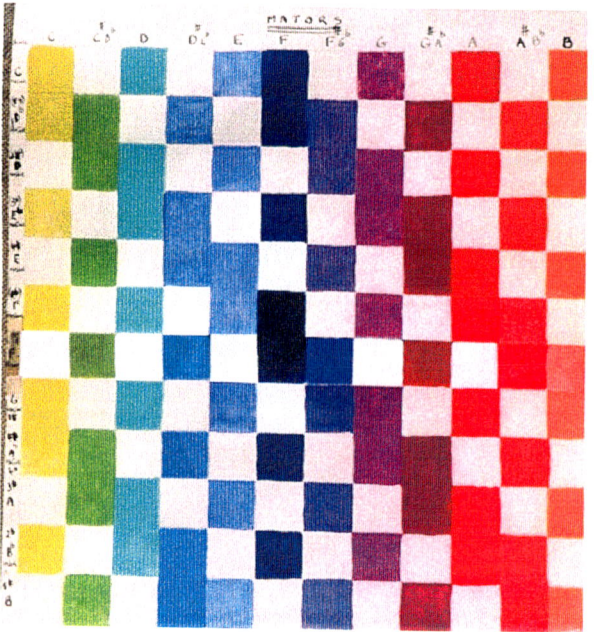

Plate 12.
Majors
(Gouache)
13 x 12.

Chapter 2.

MUSIC AND NEO-PLATONISM.

Before looking at her pictures of Landscape, Seascape & Still Life, we may turn aside to look at the influence that the Bauhaus ideas may have had upon her response in visual terms to her own first love - music. This we could term her experience of the world as she heard it.

Plate 11 'Minors', which forms a pair with 12 'Majors' [1], both presumably done at art school, are an attempt to correlate the colours of the spectrum with the octave of a major or minor musical scale. Discovering (or inventing) parallels between the visual and aural fields of perception has been a preoccupation of many composers, artists and scientists.

The concept of the 'Sister Arts' has been of interest in the sphere of philosophical aesthetics since Aristotle, Horace, and Plutarch, but has been formulated in more detail since the 18th century largely as a consequence of the contrast drawn between the activities of art and science.

1.   Ruth noted (referring to work by Roy Le Maistre) that "The Major colours of the spectrum Yellow, Green, Blue, Indigo, Violet, Red & Orange, become the scale of C Major and intervening Sharps (or Flats) lie between the appropriate colours.   In this way any major or minor scale can be read off.   The two most important notes on the musical scale - the 4th and 5th (dominant & sub-dominant) - are represented by a complementary colour, hence the choice of yellow for C.   Note the relation of the Key Note, whether cold or warm, to its important 5th & 4th.   The colour harmonics obtained retain the tone and mood of the scale.   Also note in a minor scale how the whole-tone colours make more luminous the minority values."

Goethe (1749-1832) referred memorably to architecture as 'frozen music'.

The physicist & physiologist Herman von Helmholtz (1821-94) was responsible for many advances in the field of acoustical and visual perception, and colour theorists such as Johannes Itten of the Bauhaus (ibid) and Van Ostwald also drew parallels between the wavelengths of colour and sound. The painter Kandinsky and the composer Schönberg enjoyed a rich and fruitful artistic co-operation, and the former, in his 'Concerning the Spiritual in Art', draws frequent comparisons between music and painting.

One of the earliest abstract pictures even has a musical title - Kupka's 'Amorpha, Fugue in two colours' (1912), and Klee, Delauney and Dufy were also deeply interested in this area. They may possibly have been influenced by Walter Pater who suggests in his essay 'The School of Giorgione' (1877), that all art constantly aspires towards the condition of music, in that it seeks to eliminate the distinctions between the material form and the content.

Pater, in his turn, would undoubtedly have been familiar with the work of Ruskin who, in the 'Stones of Venice' draws a cogent comparison between music and colour. A contemporary original exploration into this field is Hofstadter's 'Gödel, Esher and Bach', and other research is still in progress in the field of contemporary philosophy and physiology, notably work being done on the phenomenon of Synaesthesia.

At some point, all these analogies tend to break down because of our essentially differing perceptions of the spheres of time & space in which the two arts operate - although the quantum physicist will tell us that these two dimensions are relative to one another (and to us) so that they are, ultimately, inseparable categories. This subject has been touched on by many scientists, and Ruth possessed a copy of James Jean's 'Science and Music', which indicates her serious interest.

It is a fertile field which may yet yield greater treasures as knowledge of our perceptual relation with the world develops. For a while Ruth did, in her own way, partake of this whole fascinating area of exploration, and we can only speculate as to why she did not develop it.

One reason may have been a dearth of the kind of mutual stimulation and support that is essential for work which breaks new ground, and which by its nature is rarely an immediate commercial success. Or possibly she knew that this particular sphere was not right for her; her love of the shapes & forms, the idiosyncracies of the 'seen' world took precedence.

She is known to have painted four musical abstracts in 1977-8, 'Bach Fugue', 'Love of Three Oranges, Prokofiev', 'Musical Abstract', and 'Rachmaninov'. All were sold and unfortunately we only have (indifferent) photographs of two of them - reproduced as plates 13 & 14; neither is it known which two these are !

In plate 13 the fragments of musical notation seem to be no more than decorative devices, but they serve to direct the mind towards its intended subject. Pl 14 is more tightly knit as a composition and bears greater resemblance to a musical score.

In 1986 Ruth returned to the subject via collages (mainly) of musicians rather than music. 'The Drummer' (pl 15) even though minutely detailed is still underpinned by a coherent formal structure, with subtle gradations of tone and colour.

Plate 16 is interesting in that it develops an imagined aerial viewpoint relating to the Quintet ink sketch (17) which also formed the basis for another late collage (18). The aerial view explores the finely intersecting shapes and reciprocal stresses which are so characteristic of the chamber music sound. Its bold handling perhaps owes something to de Staël; like him, her ability to strike 'le ton juste' in colour relationships is allowed free rein when it is not constrained by illustrative demands.

This ability is matched by her gift for finding 'le mot juste' in poetic writing. As I will suggest in Part Three, Ruth's euphonius choice of words is often reminiscent of the Anglo-Welsh poetic tradition. This is evident in her one poem which specifically refers to music, but here the subject she addresses is in fact part of an even older tradition.

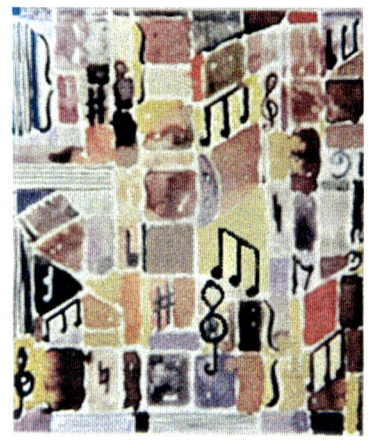

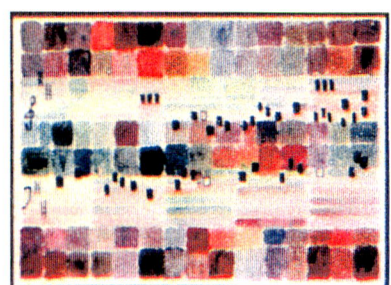

Plate 14.
Musical Abstracts.

Plate 13.

Correct picture titles & owners are unknown.

Plate 15.   The Drummer,
(Collage).

Plate 16.   Quintet, Vertical view.

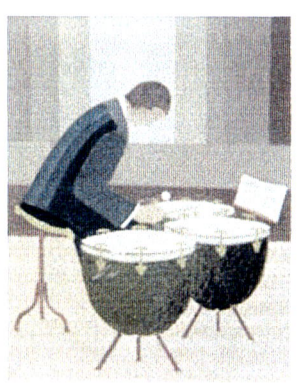

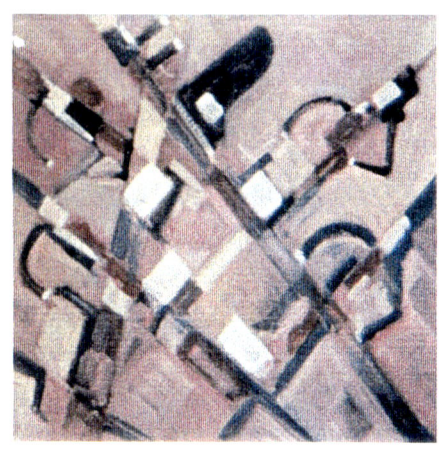

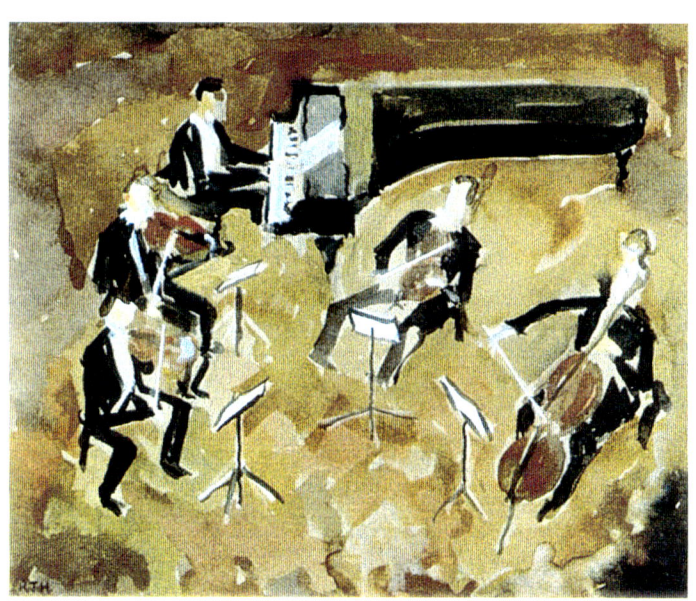

Plate 17.   Quintet   (Inks)   9 x 11.
Courtesy of Dr & Mrs G.E. Phillips.

Plate 18.   Quintet   (Collage)   7 x 8.

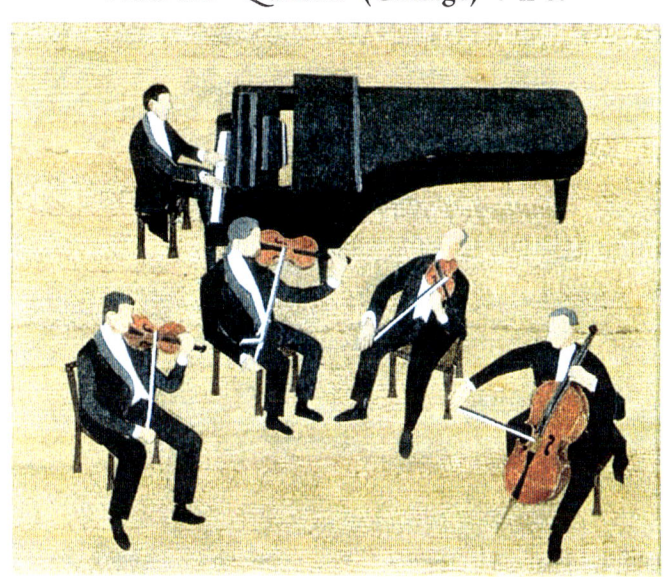

HARMONY,   by Ruth Harvey.

Exquisite music falls upon our ears
Instantly, inexorably fades - departs
To echo through the halls of space
Or circle, who can say, in widening ripples
Lost for our dimensional time
Yet lingering wistfully in imperfect memory
Faint and ill-recalled;   till we bereft
Cry to recapture, formulate, waylay
That dimly felt participation with
An all-resolving supernatural mind.

The concept of our life on earth as an anamnesis, a remembering of that which was once known on a different plane, is part of the whole fabric of philosophy. It was formulated in Western culture by Plato, but no doubt received by him from more distant sources - notably the writings of the Egyptian Hermes Trismegistus.

The idea that 'actual' music was the physical counterpart of the 'Music of the Spheres' was continued by Aristotle, Plotinus and the Medieval and Renaissance philosophers in their turn, and is frequently to be found in the works of Shakespeare.

To what extent Ruth's poem was a conscious adoption of this long tradition of Neo-Platonist thought one cannot say, but the idea that we .....

> "Cry to recapture, formulate, waylay
> That dimly felt participation with
> An all-resolving supernatural mind."

bears remarkable resemblance to, for example, the writings of Boethius. In his 'Consolations of Philosophy' - an imaginary dialogue between the writer and his Muse - the latter asks

> " .... Did the soul
> Once see the universal mind,
> And know the part, and know the whole ?"

Thirteen centuries later Wordsworth, in his Ode 'Intimations of Immortality', reveals himself as part of this tradition with the words "Our souls have sight of that immortal sea which brought us hither".

If we are indeed 'a part of all that we have met' then as well as by conscious assimilation, we also 'meet' by subconscious, intuitive absorption, ideas that are in some way the collective property of all mankind and which may, all unknown to us, already have been expressed by others.

Chapter 3.

LANDSCAPE, BUILDINGS, SEASCAPE.

Perhaps a good example to start with is 'Norchard Riding School, Manorbier' (plate 19). We have a number of charcoal drawings of this and similar scenes, from which we deduce that Ruth's instinctive interest lay with the broad organisation of simple shapes rather than with figurative detail. This manner of drawing was also partly determined by the increasing lack of mobility in her hands.

'Norchard' shows signs of a bold struggle with form which is perhaps not entirely resolved. The trees above the shed have been explored with an equal emphasis on the shapes between them, whereas the wall, gate and foreground could be part of a more figurative painting.

To abstract from nature demands a certain amount of nerve - which it all too easy to lose. However, there are some illustrious examples of paintings which display the same kind of 'split personality'; Picasso's 'Demoiselle d'Avignon' and Renoir's 'Les Parapluies' both betray such a shift in interest. The little girl in Renoir's well-known picture is still very much in the Impressionist manner, but in the umbrellas we detect a preoccupation with the underlying shapes rather than the illustrative aspect.

A more coherent and unified image is 'St Govans' (pl 20). As well as the juxtaposition of closely related blocks of colour reminiscent of the colour exercises, another possible influence is that of de Staël (see later), many of whose paintings display an interest in pure formal relationships regardless of subject.

The content of 'St. Govans' is minimal - just a headland and a horizon - but its virtue resides in the eloquent placing of shapes and the subtle gradations of tone and colour. The actual details of topography have been 'backgrounded' yet it is, remarkably, St. Govans.

The point of intersection between the sea and sky on the left hand margin lies exactly on the 'Golden Section' [1], but whether or not one has a conscious appreciation of this rightness is probably irrelevant to the satisfaction it gives. It would be interesting to know how far it was a conscious compositional ploy on Ruth's part, or whether she did it by instinct.

1.   The term 'Golden section' refers to the division of a straight line in such a way that the relation of the smaller section to the larger is the same as the larger to the whole - thus a length of, say, 8 will be divided into 3 & 5. The series progresses by adding the previous two terms together to form the next one, thus ..... 3, 5, 8, 13, 21, 34, 55, 89, etc. The ratio of these lengths is called phi (not pi) and converges on 1.618 after the first few calculations. It was codified by the 12th Century mathematician Fibonacci.

Proportions of the Fibonacci series, and particularly the spiral which is created by building up rectangles of Golden section proportion, prevail throughout nature. Their universal human appeal (and often unconscious employment in design) must be attributable to the fact that our appreciation of this inherent design in nature is due to our being ourselves a part of nature; consequently it strikes a chord in our perceptual mechanism.

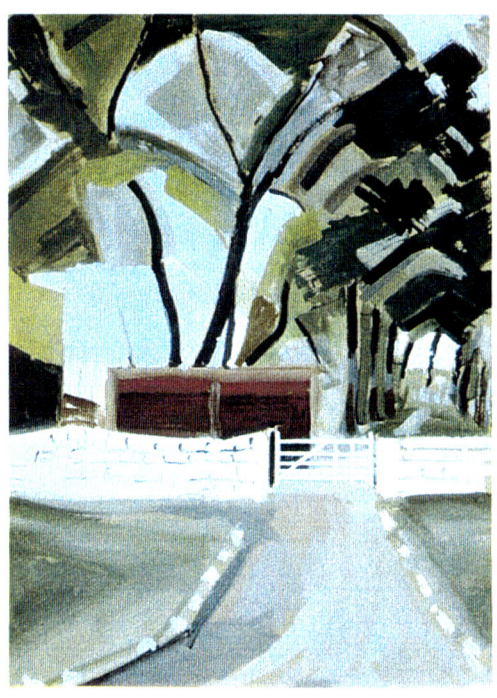

Plate 19. Norchard
       Riding School,
(Gouache) 16 x 12.

Plate 20.   St. Govans, Pembrokeshire, (Oil) 12 x 22.
Courtesy of Diana Rees.

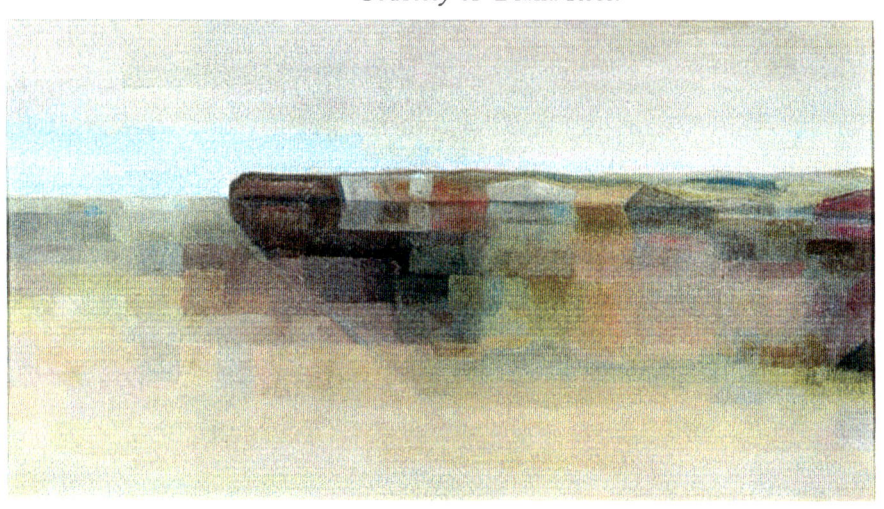

'Snow, Corhampton Down' (plate 21), is treated in a similar way, but the whole composition is more adventurous than the headland. No drawings are available of the actual scene, but we can imagine its bleakness. The subtle colour relationships are difficult to reproduce well, but are reminiscent of Klee's beautifully tuned abstractions - each block of colour finely related to its neighbour.

Plate 22, 'South Hams, Devon in Winter', again presumably derives from Ruth's experience of the landscape, and here the particular technique used to distil or transmute the actual forms again owes something to the abstract oil paintings of de Staël, such as 'Composition' (1950) or 'Landscape' (1953). His bold juxtaposition of simple shapes, which evoke the constituent elements of the landscape, would seem to be a telling influence on this picture. Ruth possessed two books on this painter, as well as a fine original lithograph and a number of cuttings and catalogues, which clearly indicate her admiration for his work.

The actual technique, broad areas of impasto laid on with a palette knife, was not one developed further by Ruth in later years, possibly because of her decreasing manual strength.

We also note that this image offers a suggestion of two alternative pathways or entrances, or 'a way not taken' - a theme which will be developed later in Part Two.

Plate 23 is another attempt to abstract from what one imagines to have been a first-hand visual experience. Like Norchard Riding School, it is not an entirely satisfactory integration between the subject and its formal treatment. The house is, as it were, still seen as a house whereas the surroundings have been reduced entirely to patterned shapes.

One should reiterate, however, that it takes an artist of the stature of Mondrian, Klee or Nicholson in their transitional periods to achieve this precarious integration, where subject is only just subject. Such paintings balance on a tightrope, and the failure to have wholly succeeded is less important than the awareness that such possibilities exist and the willingness to explore them to the best of one's abilities.

'Millmead Lock, Wey Navigation' (see plate in the Conclusion) shows how Ruth achieved her own personal synthesis - a move towards a more figurative treatment, but in terms of a quite different material - that of collage.

Another radical idea of early 20th Century art with which Ruth grappled was the distortion of space and consequent re-organisation of appearances, which was a central theme of the Italian Futurist school [2] as well as the Cubists [3].

2. The Italian Futurists - Boccione, Carra, Balla and others who flourished during the second decade of the 20th Century, pioneered the art of representing movement. Their preoccupation was with speed and dynamism, both human and mechanical, rather than the analysis of static form.

3. Cubism, contemporaneous with Futurism, was built on Cezanne's attempt to reduce all forms to the cylinder, the cone and the sphere, but abandons his use of classical perspective, introducing instead simultaneous viewpoints, as seen for example in Picasso's 'heads' which are at once full face and profile. It is an art primarily of forms which exist in their own right, not as 'second order' illustrations or approximations of reality.

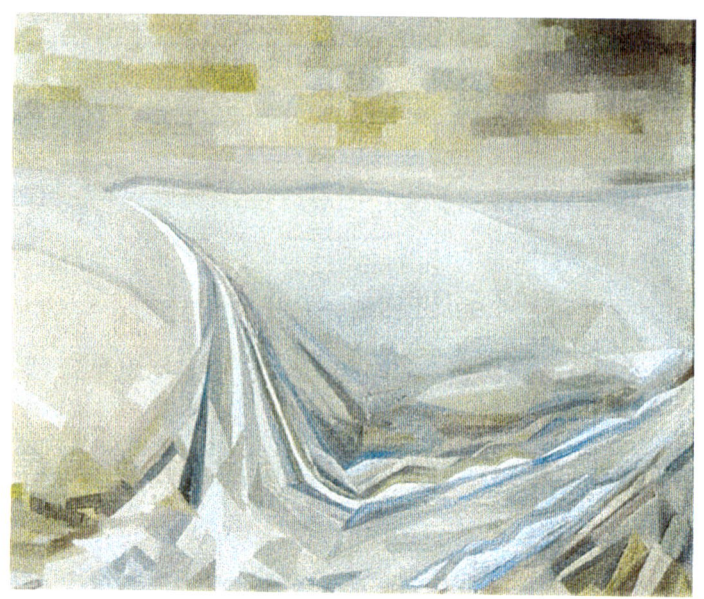

Plate 21.   Snow, Corhampton Down   (Oil)   16 x 20.

Plate 22.   South Hams, Devon, in Winter   (Oil)   21 x 37.
Courtesy of Professor & Mrs W.M. Steen.

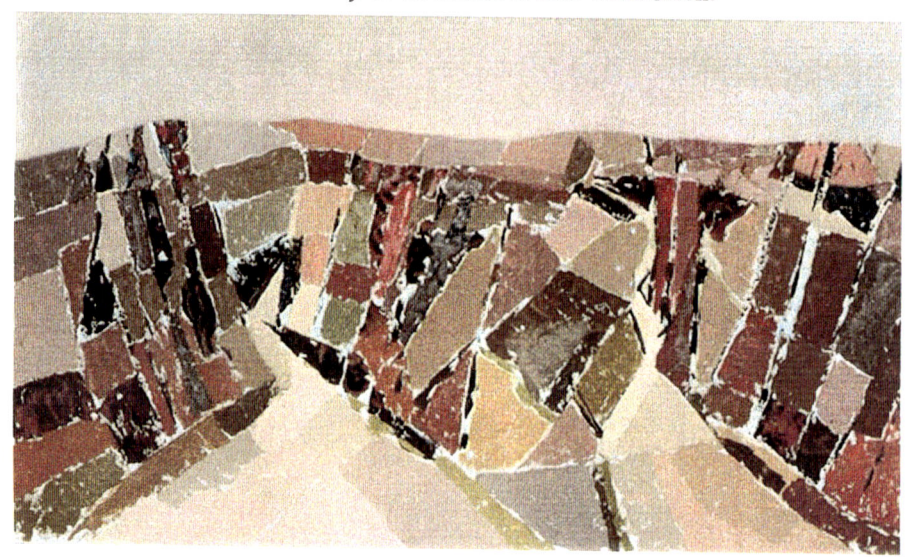

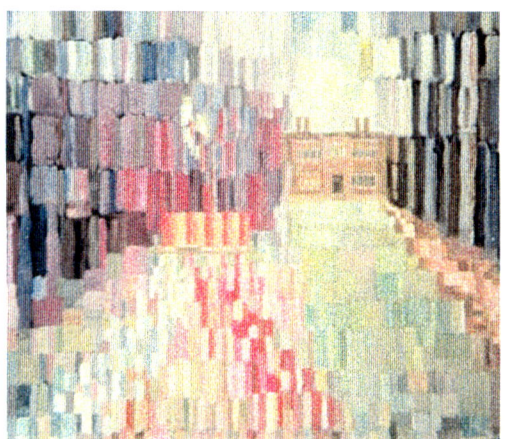

Plate 23.
House,
abstract.

Owners &
full details
of 23 & 24
unknown.

24.

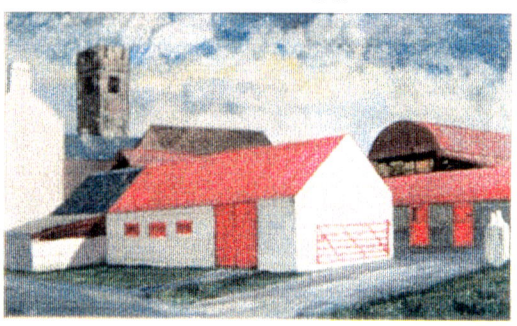

Plates 24 & 25.
Farm buildings,
St. Florence.

Pl 25 - abstract
(Inks & W-colour).
Courtesy of
Mrs M.G. McFadyen.

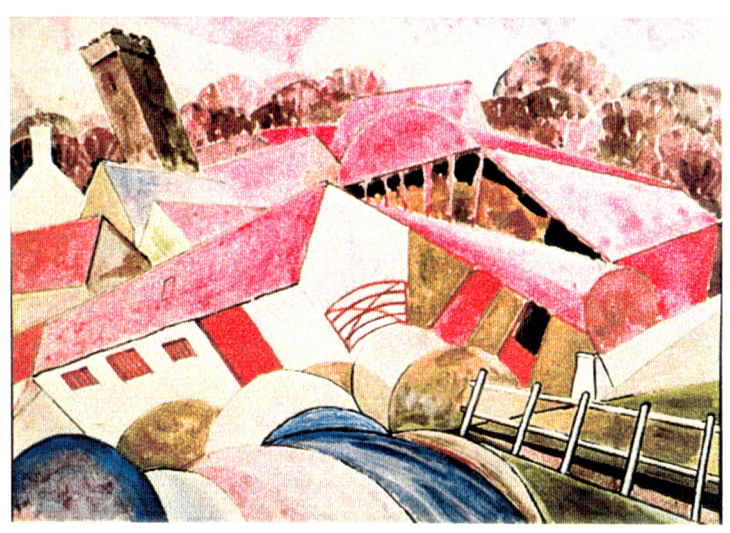

We are only aware of one example of Ruth's portrayal of this distortion of space - 'Farm Buildings, St. Florence'. The charcoal drawing (pl 26) has a vitality which is to some extent absent from the finished composition (25); the ambiguity of the sketch allows the mind a freer passage through the shapes, and the more consistent verticals give a certain stability.

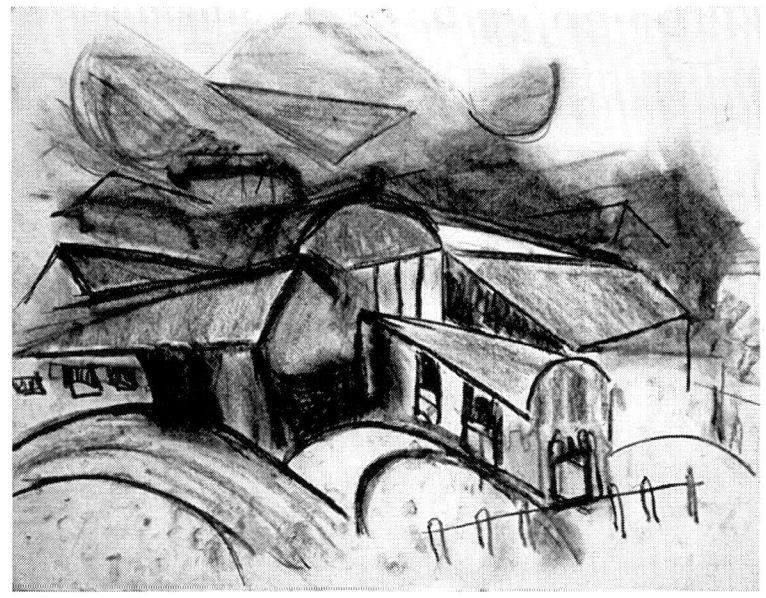

Plate 26, Farm Buildings [since demolished !],
St. Florence, abstract (drawing) 14 x 19.

The painting (25) somehow gives the impression of the after-effects of a landslip, with the buildings curiously intact, whereas the drawing explores the possibilities of distorted perspective while still retaining a sense of there being a 'ground' on which we and the buildings stand. Nevertheless, a brave attempt at this kind of art-form.

The following scenes of 'Brecon Canal' show Ruth exploring her subject by experimenting with formal devices.   In this case again the treatment is something of a cross between the early Cubists and the Futurists.   We have a number of preliminary drawings of this scene, and comparing these to the finished pictures gives insight into the means she used to simplify both the man-made structures and the landscape.

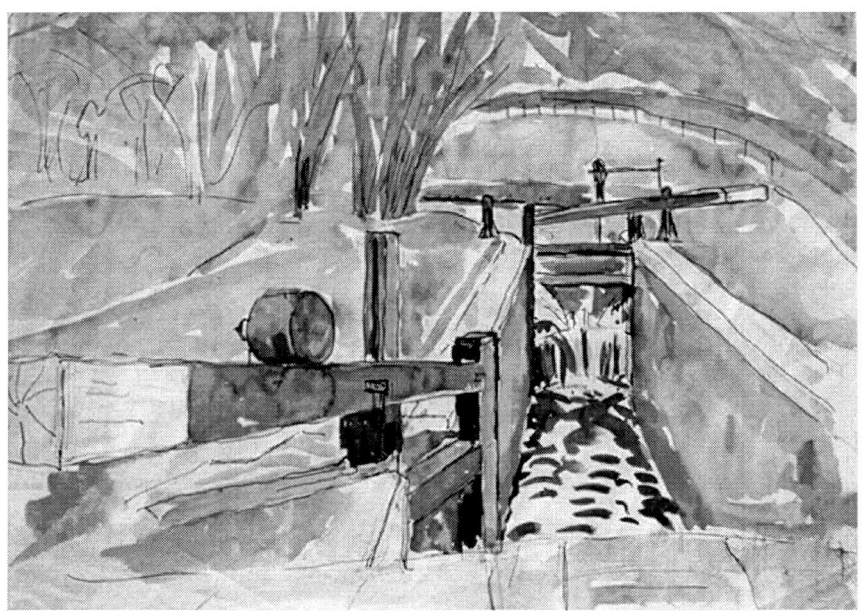

Plate 27,   Lock, filling (Ink & W-colour sketch) 14 x 19.

In both the ink pictures 28 & 29, the slightly lower viewpoint of sketch 30 has been adopted, rather than 27, thereby giving the whole composition the benefit of a more acute diagonal.

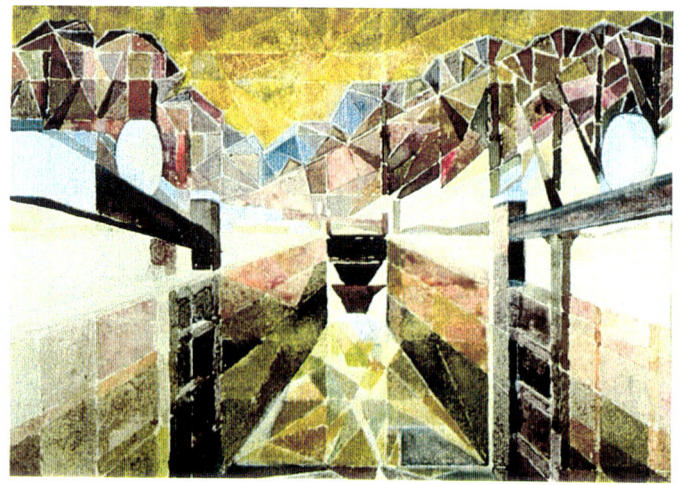

Plate 28.   Lock, abstract (Watercolour & Inks) 13 x 20.
Plate 29.   Lock, Brecon Canal (Inks) H x W 22 x 16.
Plate 30.   Lock, empty (Charcoal & Wash) 19 x 13.

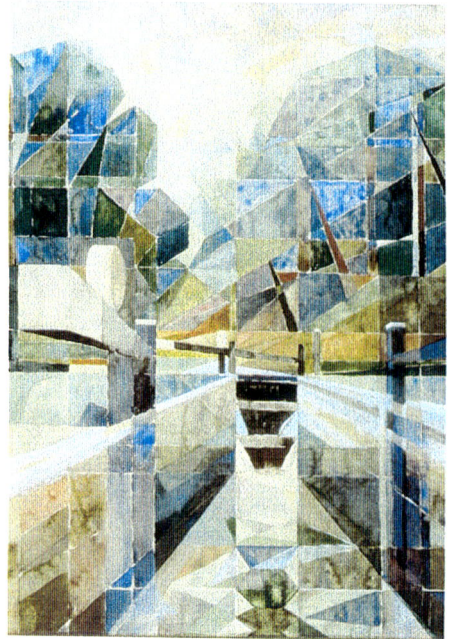

Sketch - plate 30.

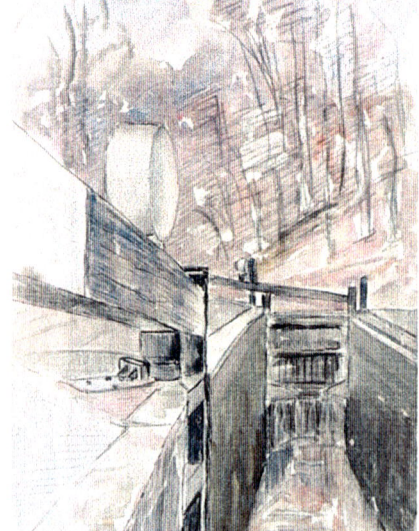

This is where the painter's eye and mind take precedence over that of the photographer - she is not limited to any one precise moment; the subject (or similar subjects) may be revisited on any number of occasions and from this cumulative experience an image can be made which expresses the most characteristic aspects of the subject. We do not know which picture came first, but I would hazard a guess that even if they were done quite separately Ruth had the other in mind, to allow her to emphasize different aspects of the scene.

In pl 28 the background trees seem to have exercised her mind somewhat, and because of their laborious patterning they tend to come forward and demand our attention. This creates a certain conflict with the solid area of the lock structure which is expressed more convincingly in plate 28, while in 29 the cool blues & greens make it more mobile and ambiguous.

In both pictures the problem seems to be integrating the different parts of the scene - building and trees - into a coherent formal whole. The diagonals of the background hill have been strongly felt and deconstructed in terms of rigid rectilinear shapes; but because their actual shapes have been differently felt from the mechanical ones seen, as it were, under a different rubric, the synthesis in formal terms has not been entirely achieved.

I suggest that in plate 28 particularly there is a kind of 'split' between lock and trees, and in both cases the lower half is the more successful, partly because the man-made structure lends itself more naturally to Cubism. Plate 29 is more integrated and offers a delicately ambiguous play of shape and colour.

Chapter 4.

STILL LIFE and ARTEFACTS.

In addition to the plates following, many illustrations of this subject area appeared in Volume I. For the most part, Ruth seems to have had no need to treat them in an abstract way, as if the recording of their actual shapes, a kind of homage to their textures, colours and construction was enough.

The mushrooms on plate 32 have been carefully and evenly arranged, each one treated with the same intensity of detail, and with little indication of their setting or any secondary motifs to detract from them.

Similar in approach are the cherries and greengages (pls 31 & 33). Ruth made many such studies of a whole range of fruit in different containers, experimenting with various viewpoints and sometimes indicating the setting, sometimes not.

The pictures where the background is blank allow us to focus on the subjects, and are arguably more successful than those where the background has been filled up. In 'Wasp Jar' (38) the whole picture is fully integrated, with both jar and table-cloth seen and painted as a whole, and the subtle colour scheme is enlivened by a daring touch of red in the upper right-hand corner.

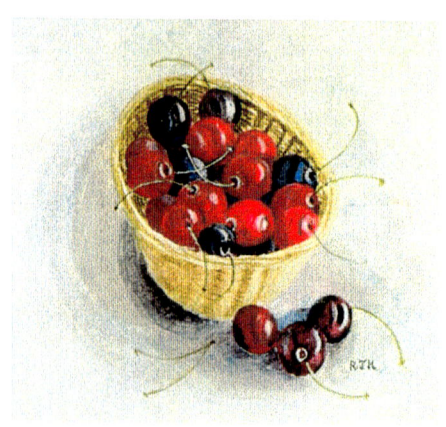

Plate 31.   Cherries in
Wicker Basket,
(Watercolour, Inks &
Bodycolour) 6 x 7.

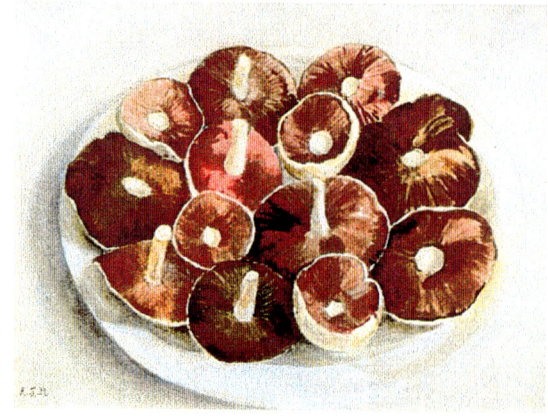

Plate 32. Mushrooms,
(Watercolour) 7 x 10.

Plate 33.   Greengages,
(Watercolour & Inks)
5 x 6.

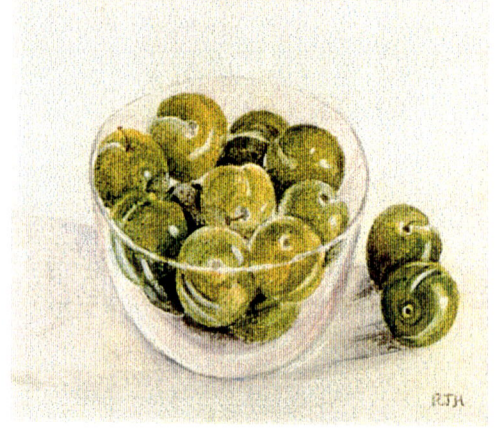

In 'Still Life with Bottles' (pl 40 [1]), the delicate placing of the shapes - both of the objects and also the equally important spaces in between, is reminiscent of de Staël or Nicholson. One of Ruth's books on the former shows a painting of kitchen scales, which was nevertheless contemporaneous with works devoid of subject matter - along with other artists of the early 20th Century, de Staël worked both figuratively and abstractly.

Some words of Barbara Hepworth [2] express why *she* needs to engage in both kinds of work ;   "Working realistically replenishes ones's love for life, humanity and the earth. Working abstractly seems to release one's personality and sharpen the perceptions, so that in the observation of life it is the wholeness or inner intention which moves one so profoundly".

Anyone who has attempted to work abstractly will appreciate the aptness of this remark, but also, learning to *perceive* abstract work has the effect of sharpening our perception of the stresses and relationships that can be discovered below the surface of things seen.

1.   Previously printed on a larger scale in Volume I.
2.   Quoted in 'The Meaning of Art', Herbert Read, Penguin 1949, p189.

However, maritime artefacts seemed not to point Ruth to anything beyond themselves - "wonderfully and marvellously made" these studies seem to say ... and if we feel them to be beautiful then this resides in their having been designed for, and fulfilling a very specific purpose - they are totally and elegantly functional.

But it takes the artist, whose interest is 'disinterested' - in that he is not primarily concerned with their efficiency - to bring to our attention how marvellous these things actually are, thus enhancing their status beyond that of the merely useful.

'Buoys, Swansea Docks' (plate 34) in particular achieves a monumental quality by virtue not only of the accomplished drawing but of the subtle range of colour and controlled tonal relations. Turn the picture upside down, and this play of stress and counter-stress will be apparent.

The full frontal oil 'Propeller' (plate 35) is another outright celebration of the beauty of a manufactured article which perfectly fulfils its purpose.

Unusual or abandoned and rusting farm machinery captured Ruth's attention, also such things as the 'Old Petrol Pump' (36); likewise cranes, derricks and all sorts of smaller quayside artefacts, summarised beautifully in the montage 'Bollards, Milford Docks' (37).

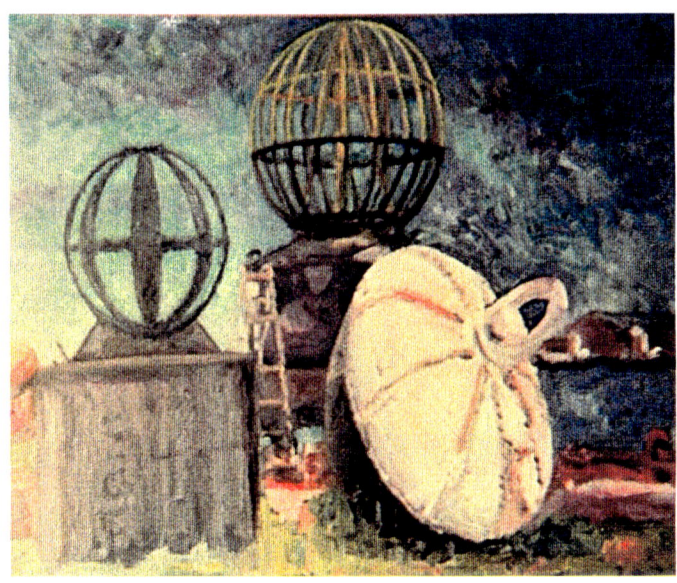

Plate 34.   Buoys, Swansea Docks (Gouache).   *Owner unknown.*
Plate 35.   Propeller (Oil) 14 x 14.   *Courtesy of Mr & Mrs H. Davies.*

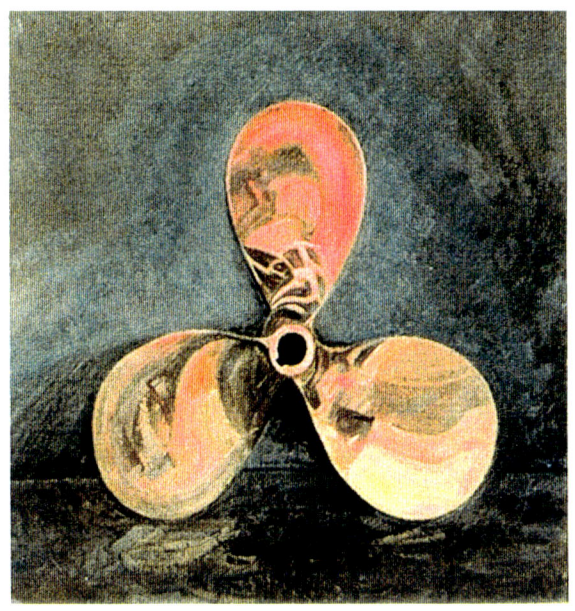

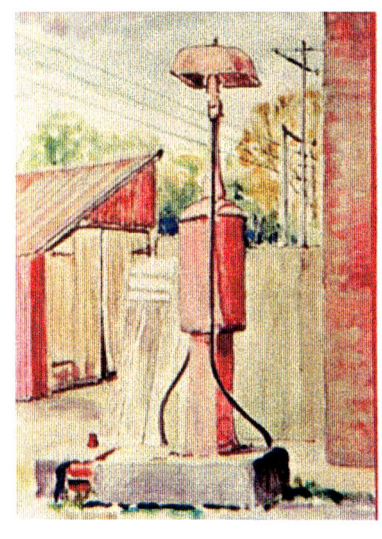

Plate 36.   Old Petrol Pump.

Owner and full details unknown.

Plate 37.   Bollards, Milford Docks (Watercolour) 11 x 16.

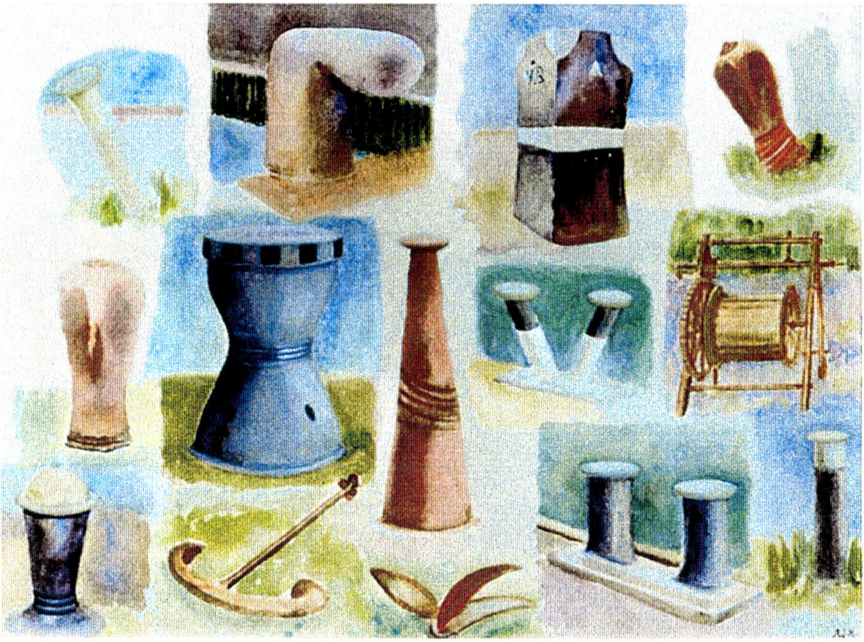

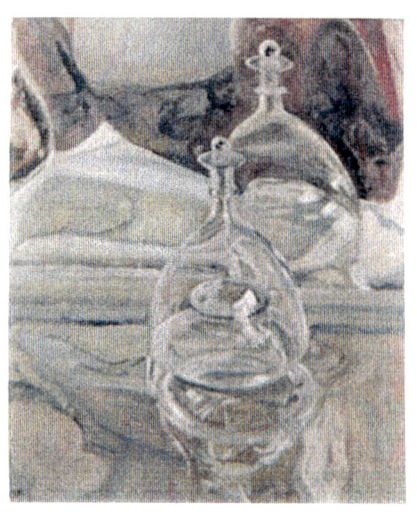

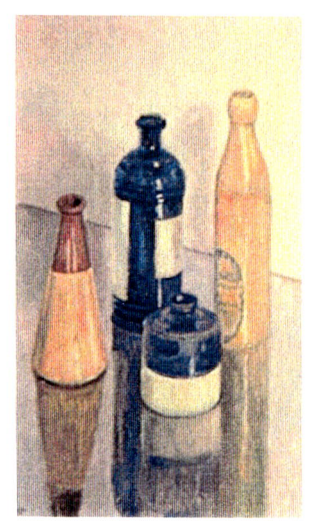

Plate 38.   Wasp Jar.

Plate 39.   Bottles &
Owners and details of 38 & 39 unknown.   Flower Jars.

Plate 40.   Still Life with Bottles (Oil) 18 x 26.
Courtesy of Mr & Mrs R.H.B. Edwards.

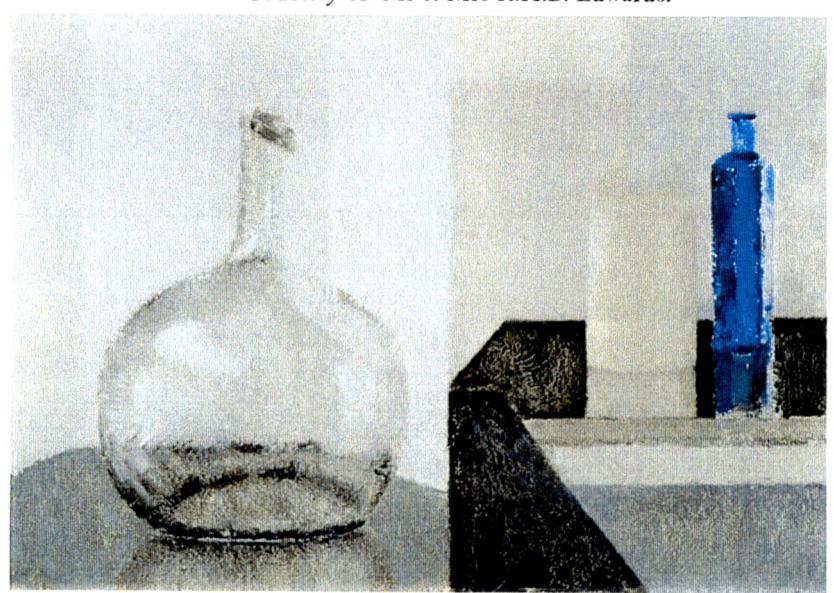

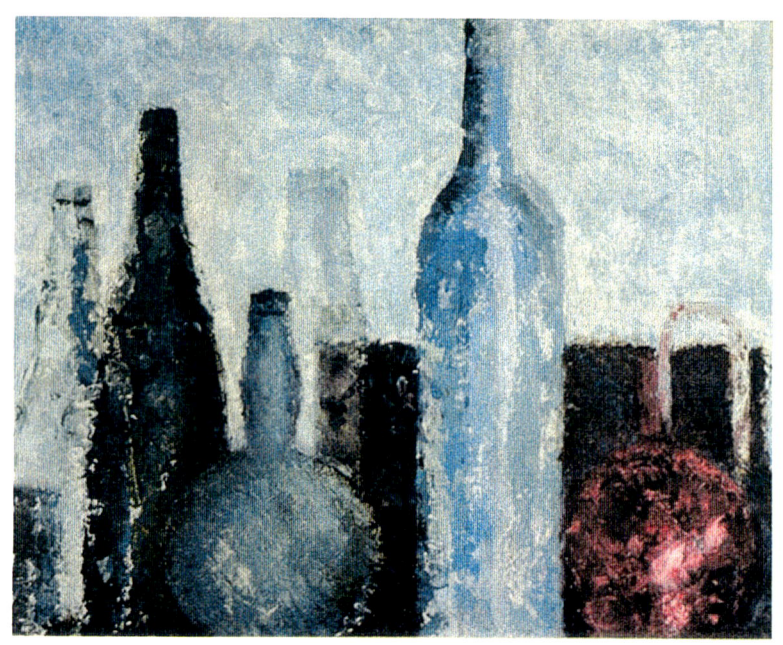

Plate 41.
Bottles (Oil),
    14 x 17.
Courtesy of
Robert Hunter.

Plate 42.
Blue Glass Bottles,
(Watercolour)
H x W   8 x 6.

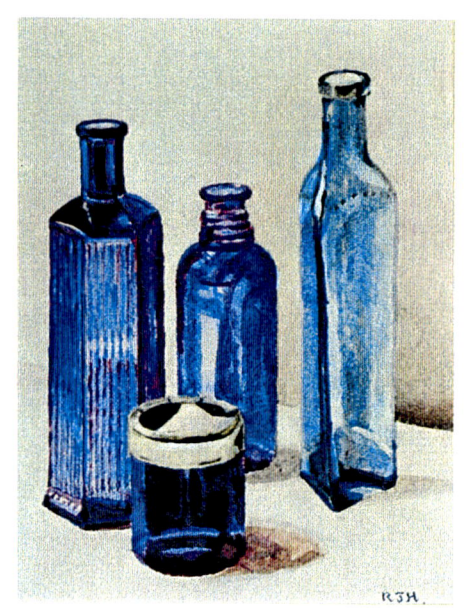

As well as the 'Still Life with Bottles' (40) mentioned, we have another early oil on this same theme - 'Bottles' (plate 41). Ruth was clearly influenced by the work of Morandi whose treatment elevates them beyond being merely bottles, yet allows them to retain their essential character.

This tightly clustered group of bottles makes no concession to an illusion of depth or modelling of individual forms. Its strength lies in the flat pattern, and the way our eye is led round and across the shapes. The placing of the tallest bottle's left hand edge is, again, precisely on the golden section, and the surprising way in which its top is truncated by the frame ensures that our eye immediately rebounds towards the other shapes.

By contrast to the robust handling of 41, 'Blue Glass Bottles' (42) is a move towards greater representation of tactile surfaces. We imagine that it was done after the two oils just discussed, which emphasises again that an artist's progress is not always in a steady direction; intuitive forays into abstraction may be followed by a need to reassert and celebrate the sensible appearance of things.

The actuality of this glassware is strikingly rendered. We are reminded precisely of the subtle nuances of colour and texture of such things - again produced for purely utilitarian purposes. Plate 39 is another case in point.

'Bottles & Chemistry Set' (plate 43) seems to fall somewhere between these two, with both an interest in the shape of the containers as well as the textures of the glasses. 'Still Life with Rose' (44) tends towards a more consciously decorative manner, and we detect an interest in the shapes of the bottle, and its reflection on the table, which could develop in the same way as the Brecon locks. The handling of the paint here is beautifully crisp and elegant, as befits the subject.

'Bottle and view to Field' (pl 45) was found amongst Ruth's loose portfolio bundle, which implies that she did not consider it good enough to be framed.   Nevertheless, it is a bold and atmospheric study with a beautifully controlled harmony of closely related colours.   In many ways it is reminiscent of the work of Winifred Nicholson or Duncan Grant, reproductions of whose works appear in many of her reference books.

A 'finished' version also exists, with a cooler colour scheme, which to my mind lacks the robust handling of the study, as if the care taken with tidying up the composition inhibited the flow of brush and paint.   Also, this version may have been done from the sketch and away from the subject - and therefore without the stimulation of the actual scene.

A subsequent attempt to recapture in paint something seen and recorded at the time - a 'recollection in tranquillity' - often demands the stimulus of a different material to revitalise the subject, to bring it back to life again, which, as we will see, is precisely what happens in Ruth's later collages.

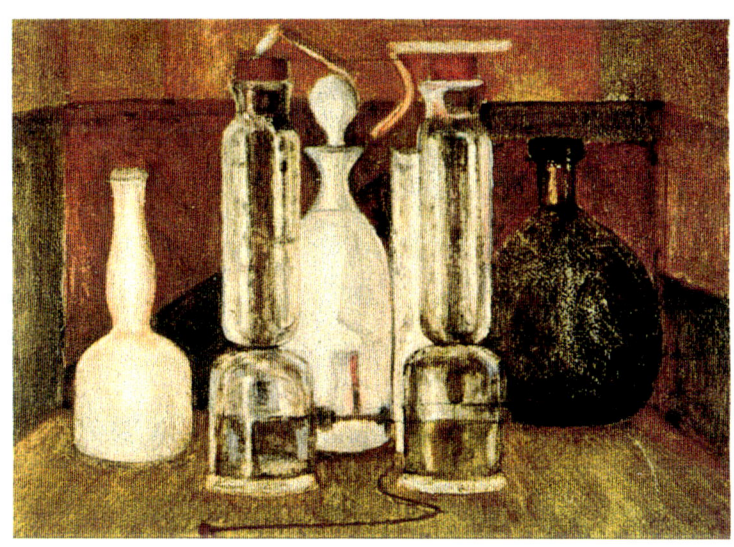

Plate 43.   Bottles & Chemistry Set   (Oil)   20 x 28.
Plate 44.   Still Life with Rose   (Inks)   13 x 9.
            Courtesy of Mr & Mrs G.M. Hunter.
Plate 45.   Bottle and view to Field   (Gouache)   21 x 16.

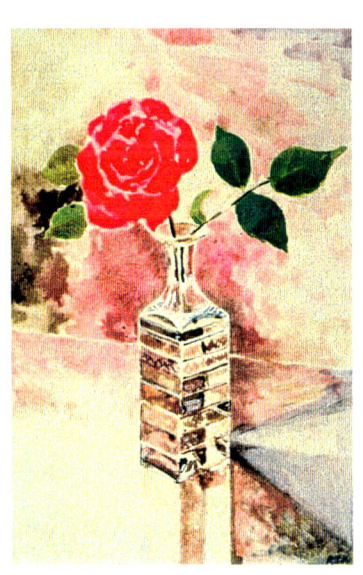

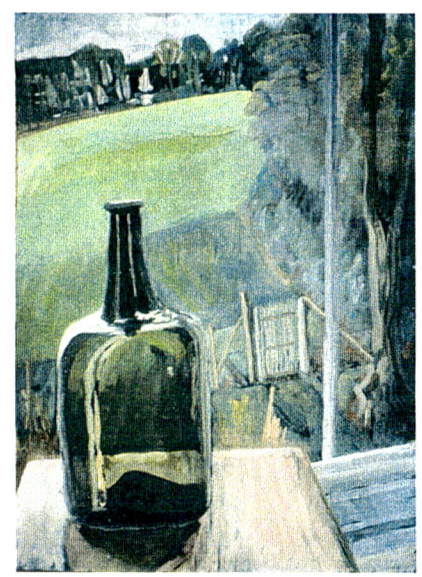

Chapter 5.

OTHER INFLUENCES & SOURCES.

Ruth amassed a considerable library of books on art which reflected her particular taste and interests. These comprise for the most part works by 20th Century artists, notably Ben & Winifred Nicholson, the Nash brothers, William Scott, David Hockney, de Staël and Mondrian.

As well as monographs on these and other individuals, she possessed a number of books on groups such as the St. Ives artists and the English Post-Impressionists, together with the Tate and Courtauld Galleries' collections, and numerous other gallery catalogues.   Over the years she also collected whole boxes of cuttings which she filed under various headings.

For the artist living and working outside the mainstream, the need to contact and refer to the work of others is especially important.   Ruth clearly felt this need and steadily accumulated a rich store of references which could best help her develop her own vision in the absence of the direct encouragement and advice of other artists.

She was also interested in the 18th & 19th Century English Water-colourists and possessed several volumes on John Sell Cotman and Thomas Rowlandson.   The former's sturdy yet lyrical chalk drawings (many of which are in the British Museum) arouse our instant admiration.   When we compare them with his more finished watercolours, such as Greta Bridge or Durham Cathedral, we can appreciate how the studies have been refined and invested with a formal authority which is not always apparent in the tradition of British landscape.

This aspect interests us in relation to Ruth's work because it is precisely this sense of structural probity that we find in her own later collages.   She was obliged, to some extent, to question and reappraise her technique, and refine her means in response to both her vision and her physical limitations.

Among the other artists she admired were Eric Ravilious and Edward Bowden, early 20th Century painters whose interests tended towards 'illustration' rather than the more austerely formal work of the Bauhaus group.   She also had a signed volume by John Piper.

These few names tell us that - at least when these books were acquired - Ruth was keenly interested in ways of depicting and commenting on the world in a figurative way; however, that her final mode of expression did not develop in this direction may be due to many different causal factors.

She shared a particular interest in Welsh Chapels with John Piper, but stylistically her treatment of them does not seem to bear much relation to his. Unfortunately we have no (good enough) examples available to reproduce, which must indicate that they were sold quickly. It also seems that she was content to record them in terms of paint, as it does not appear that she developed any of them into collages.

As well as volumes on other artists she possessed a number of books and pamphlets which reflect topographical or subject-matter interest. A great many of these tell us how interested she was in the construction of man-made objects; windows, doors, industrial archeology, chapel architectures, domestic artefacts, canals & locks. She also collected material relating to the landscape, particularly parts of the country with which she felt an affinity, and many of her late collages also feature scenes which she had seen and studied many years earlier.

In later years she frequently painted subjects not encountered at first hand but taken from some of her innumerable cuttings. 'The Swarm' and 'Hunting for Truffles' (both in Volume I) seem to have been inspired by newspaper photographs, and her collage 'The Paddlers' (pl 81) is definitely developed from an old photograph in an art book on beach & seaside scenes [1].

That Ruth felt the need to explore subjects not available to her 'live' was probably due to her decreasing mobility.

1.   The Beach, Geoffrey Dutton, Oxford University Press, 1985, p36.

PART TWO

Plate 46.   Lake at Stackpole,
(Oil) 18 x 18.   *Courtesy of*
Mr & Mrs R.H.B. Edwards.

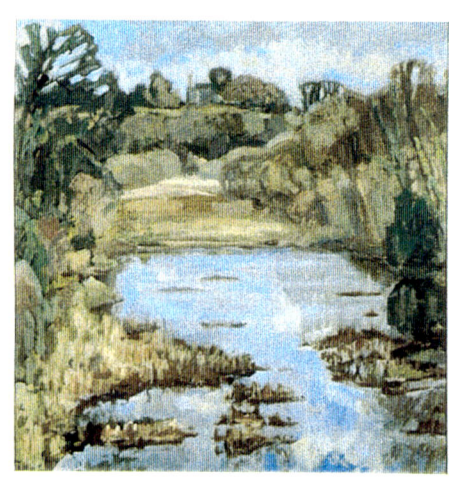

Plate 47.   Dartmouth,
(Oil) 12 x 24.
Courtesy of Joan Cowburn.

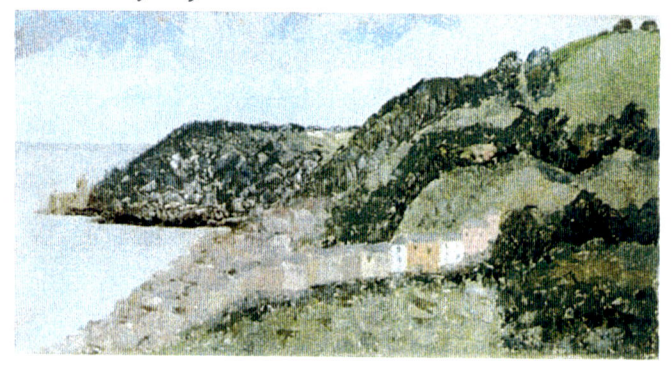

Plate 48.   Slate Quarries in Preseli Hills,
(Oil, 1970) 15 x 29.   *Courtesy of Mrs H.L. Underwood.*

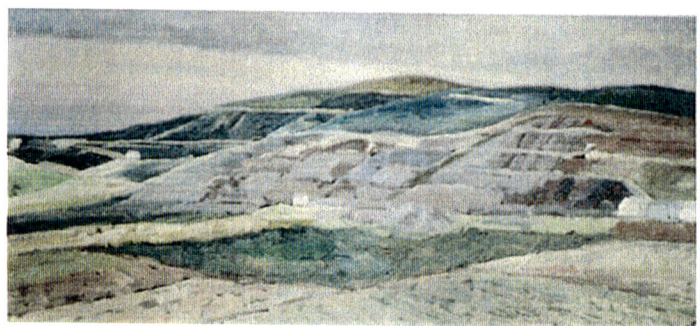

THE TRANSITION FROM PAINTING TO COLLAGE.

We begin by looking back at three of Ruth's early oil paintings. These pictures probably date from the early 1970's.

The robust handling of 'Lake at Stackpole' (plate 46) is particularly reminiscent of some of the more straightforward English Post-Impressionists such as the Camden Town group, whom Ruth obviously admired as much as those artists whose interests veered more towards formalism.

We imagine they were all painted from life; 'Stackpole' and 'Dartmouth' (pl 47) show no conscious inclination to reduce the scene to a formal design, but in the 'Slate Quarries' (48) we can detect an interest in the subtle intersections of the hillsides which would be developed in many later collages.

Before moving on to these collages we need to look at the part played by the actual *material* in any work of art and the reciprocal influence it has upon the idea in the artist's mind, and also at the notion of 'style'.

As regards material, Ruth was clearly excited by the textures and subtle colours of handmade papers, and copies of several letters were found addressed to 'Paperchase' in London which listed her exact requirements. I once gave her some samples that I had hoarded for many years and never used. Her delight in them was evident, and she immediately visualised their potential - "this one would be marvellous for a ploughed field ..... that one lends itself to a pebbly beach", etc.

In one of Ruth's many catalogues from the Crane Kalman gallery [1], Alan Ross quotes some words of Ben Nicholson ..... "To be fully alive, an artist's idea and the material he's working with must become inseparable; fighting against the material is as good a way as any of becoming totally involved".

'Fighting' is an apt word. For what we have in any art work is not a tree, or a house, or a person, but those things *under the form of the material,* and it is this which is responsible for the work's aesthetic character. To achieve a unity of idea and material, where the medium becomes the subject and the subject is re-born, as it were, *through* the material, always involves a struggle. Ruth visualised her subjects through these papers, and in doing so achieved her own personal means of expressing what she saw, felt and imagined.

The best of her late collages achieve a magical metamorphosis whereby, for instance, the eddies of an estuary *become* the paper, as the paper *becomes* the eddies; and yet in virtue of this mysterious alchemy they still remain themselves. The essential character of each is enhanced rather than diminished.

1.   Ben Nicholson : Early Works, Crane Kalman, London, May 1968.

Part One looked at the way Ruth explored and assimilated to some extent many of the new ideas of early 20th Century art, but without arriving at a particular style of her own.   To conclude this preamble to a study of her more mature work, the word 'style' in itself may benefit from some explanation.

It is derived from the Latin 'stilus', a writing instrument, and has come to mean not only the individual calligraphic flourishes whereby graphologists can deduce our character traits, but an overall individuality of expression whether in the things we create such as pictures, gardens and home decor, or simply the way we move, dress and speak.

We leave some trace of our uniqueness on all that we make. The *self* will 'seep through' even the most accomplished (technically) work, and in the visual arts it is that intangible element which, if sufficiently developed, clearly distinguishes one artist from another even if their materials and subject-matter are identical. The degree to which an individual artist possesses 'style' is dependent upon a clear and unique vision, and a sound technique totally in tandem with that vision.

A historical style such as the International Gothic, or Rococco, for example, arises out of the accumulated interplay of whole generations of artists with the prevailing Zeitgeist (or spirit of the age) which in turn has evolved from the vision-plus-technique of previous generations.

Having seen 'Slate Quarries' where the abstraction process (so to speak) did not reach its logical conclusion in a more formal work, and having discussed briefly the implications of material and style, we are now in a position to look at several subjects which Ruth did develop into collages.

A subject which embraces the gradual transition to her own particular method is 'Drive to Blackawton'. Pathways and entrances to woods were a recurring theme in her work, but this particular scene provides an interesting paradigm for the development of a personal vision.

The charcoal drawing (plate 49) is typical of Ruth's vigorous and simplified approach to nature.

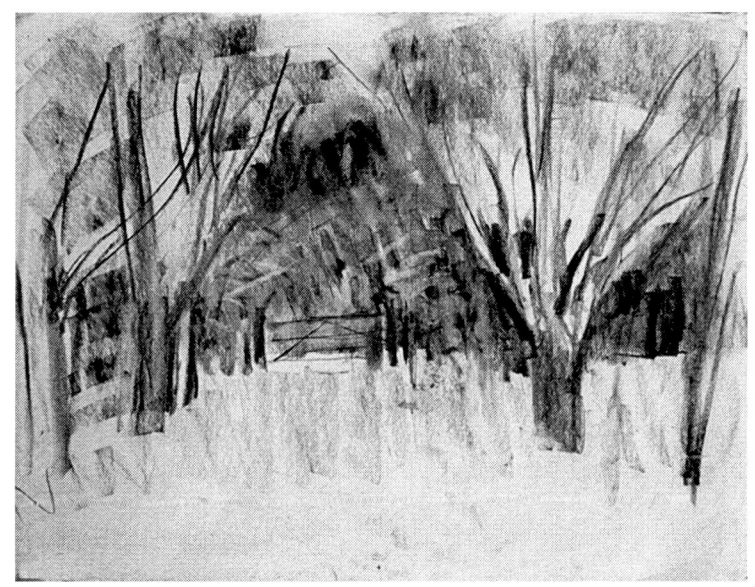

Plate 49.   Drive to Blackawton (Drawing) 14 x 19.

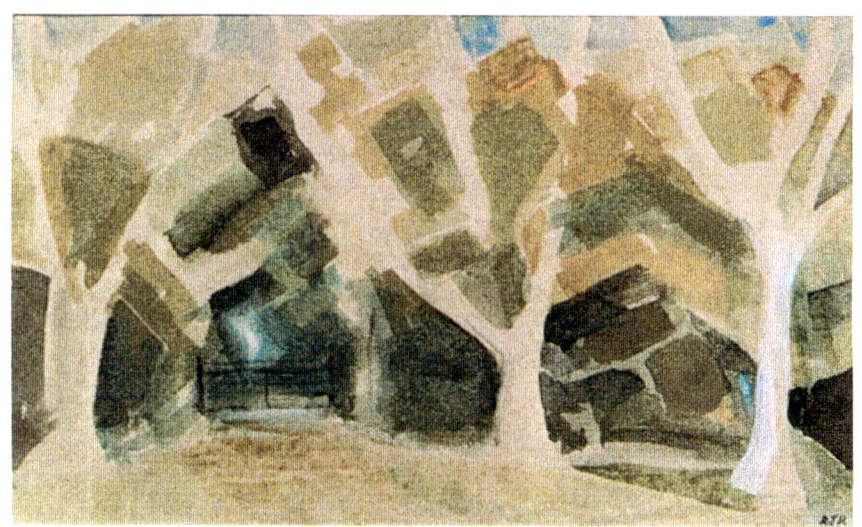

Plate 50.   Drive to Blackawton (Watercolour) 10 x 16.

Plate 51.   Drive to Blackawton (Collage) 8 x 10.

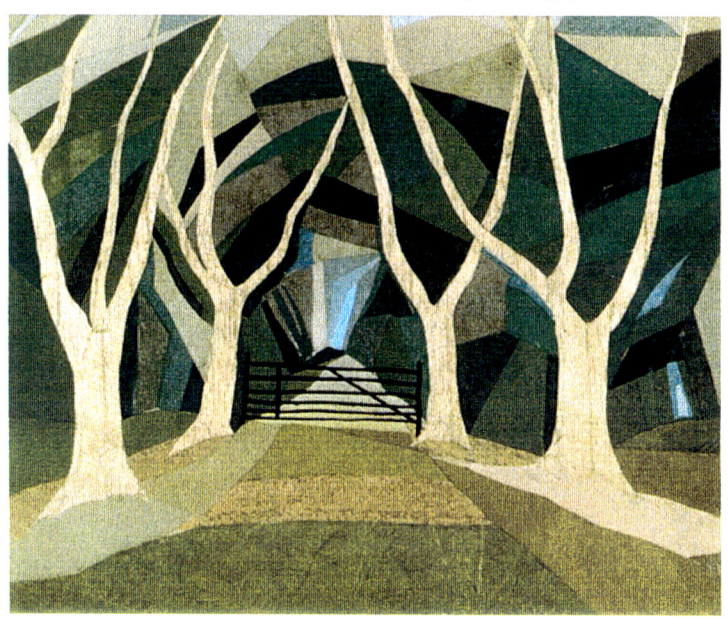

The watercolour (with some gouache, plate 50) attempts further simplification of the natural forms, and would appear to be influenced by Cezanne's approach to similar woodland scenes, as well as by early works of Braque. Here the structure is of paramount importance rather than the transient effects of light, or the subjective sensations aroused by the scene, which find expression in romantic exaggeration.

The concern here is with the ordering of visual impression in the pursuit of greater simplicity and coherence. Such scenes, as one knows, are full of minute details, shimmering nuances of light, textures and colours which could easily become congested when translated into paint.

It is interesting that in this picture, as in 'Norchard', the gate appears to be a stumbling block in that it is not treated in the same broad manner as the trees. It is still 'a gate'.

When we move on to look at the collage (pl 51), we can see that this certain inconsistency in treatment is still apparent. The relationship between the tree trunks has been changed, and the placing of the two glimpses of light altered, both in their relation to the trunks and to the whole area of the image. My personal view is that the right hand glimpse is more satisfyingly placed in the watercolour - enclosed between two trees - whereas in the collage it seems to be below ground level.

However, the whole impression is one of subtle mystery - the simple shapes giving a cave-like quality.   The idea of an alternative path through the wood, which is further developed in pl 75 (see also Vol I for a larger print) where the two options are given equal emphasis, was also of interest to Ruth, as well as the purely formal problems.

I was reminded of Robert Frost's poem 'The Road not taken', and wondered whether Ruth knew it.   On looking through her many poetry books I came across a volume of Frost's collected works; on the inside cover she had noted three poems - and this was one.   The first few lines will suffice .....

> "Two roads diverged in a yellow wood,
>   And sorry I could not travel both
>   And be one traveller, long I stood
>   And looked down one as far as I could
>   To where it bent in the undergrowth;"

Ruth's folders of cuttings also yielded 'The Way through the Woods' by Rudyard Kipling, and next to it a poem by Edwin Muir 'The Way', whose theme is similar :-

> "Friends, I have lost the way
>   The way leads on.
>   Is there another way ? ..... "

The trouble she took to copy these works, and very many others, indicates how wide was her field of interest.

Returning to Ruth's art, there are several other subjects which figured recurringly.

Examples of making the most of a good subject occur in all the arts. However, what constitutes a 'good' subject is in itself subjective. The artist or poet can alert us to qualities in quite ordinary scenes or events which take us - as they took him - beyond the mundane actuality.

This transfiguration of the commonplace is one of the greatest values of the arts, where a seemingly everyday event acquires an unprecedented significance and numinosity through the maker's ability to find the right form for his vision.

In an apparently unselfconscious process, artists become drawn to certain subjects by virtue of an intuitive empathy which cannot always be explained. Alfred Wallis' boats, Winifred Nicholson's flowers, David Jones' window vistas or Ceri Richard's pianists all startle us into re-appraising their subject, and enable us to dare to see the world like that.

Inevitably some subjects begin to recur more frequently, and one may draw a comparison with a composer reusing a good theme in different disguises in different works, or even in a different context in the same work.

'Bozzom Zeal, Devon' (the actual picture titles vary as shown), provides another interesting paradigm for the developmental process; by looking at this series of four works we can trace the way her interest moved under the influence of the material, and come to see what was lost and what was gained by it.

We imagine that the watercolour study (pl 52) may have been the earliest work, probably during the 1960's, because it is similar in style to many other sketches she made on the spot. No attempt is made to radically re-order the shapes of the landscape, or emphasise some parts at the expense of others. The colours are closely harmonious.

Plates 53 & 54 are very similar - a slightly higher viewpoint in both - though the boat has been omitted in 54. The charcoal study clearly defines the curve of the central hill as it turns into the creek, but in the oil this sense of 3-dimensions is less important than the sense of rhythmic patterning created by the field shapes.

The final collage (plate 55) reverts to the lower viewpoint - which lends a more striking silhouette to the central hilltop, and here there is no attempt to create an illusion of depth in space. The various graining of the papers add to the surface design by creating diagonal or vertical stress within the shapes.

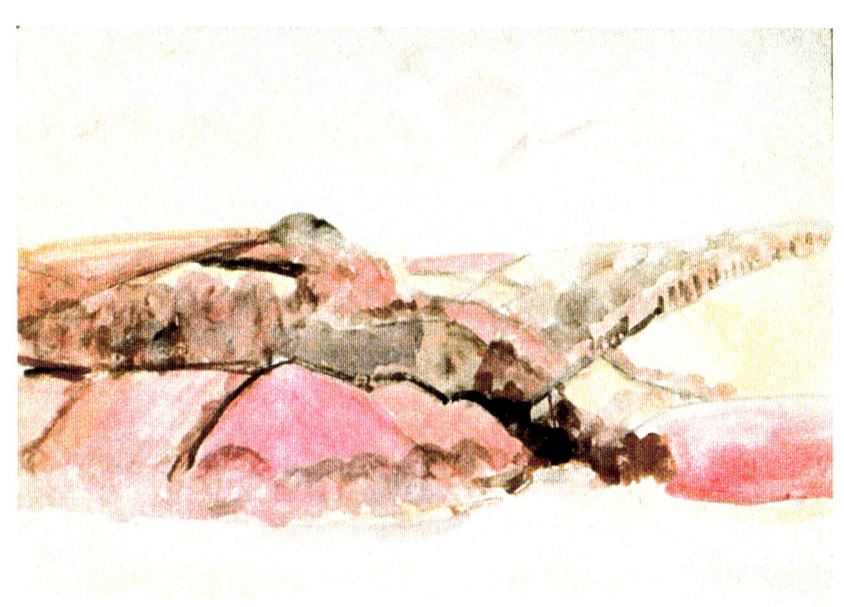

Plate 52.   Dittesham Creek, Dartmouth   (Watercolour) 13 x 19.

Plate 53.   Dittesham Creek, Dartmouth   (Charcoal sk.) 12 x 18.
Courtesy of Mr & Mrs R.H.B. Edwards.

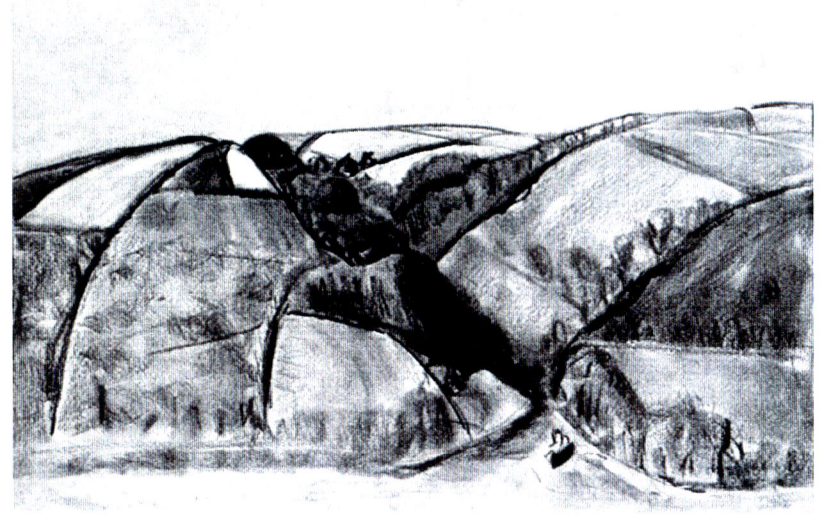

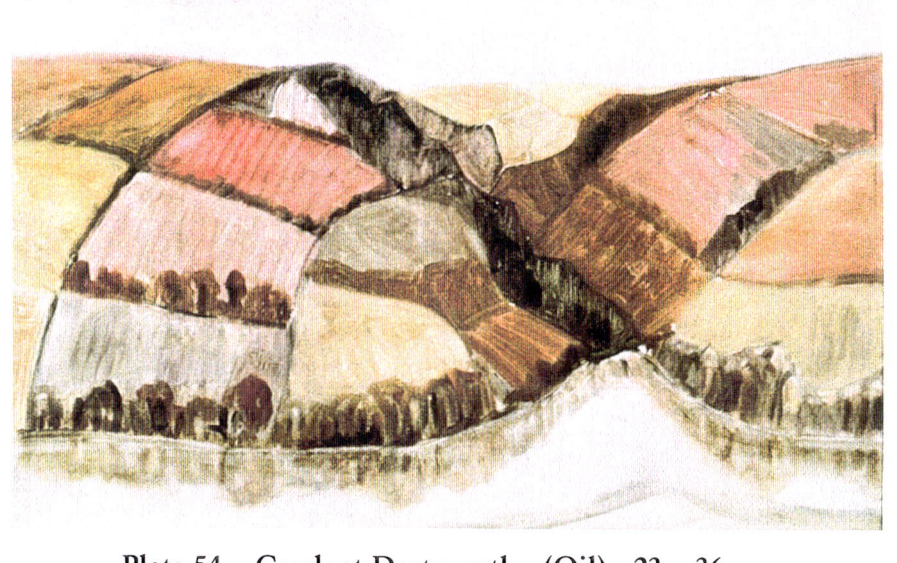

Plate 54.   Creek at Dartmouth   (Oil)   23 x 36.
Courtesy of Mr & Mrs R.H.B. Edwards.
Plate 55.   Bozzom Zeal, Devon (Collage) 16 x 20.

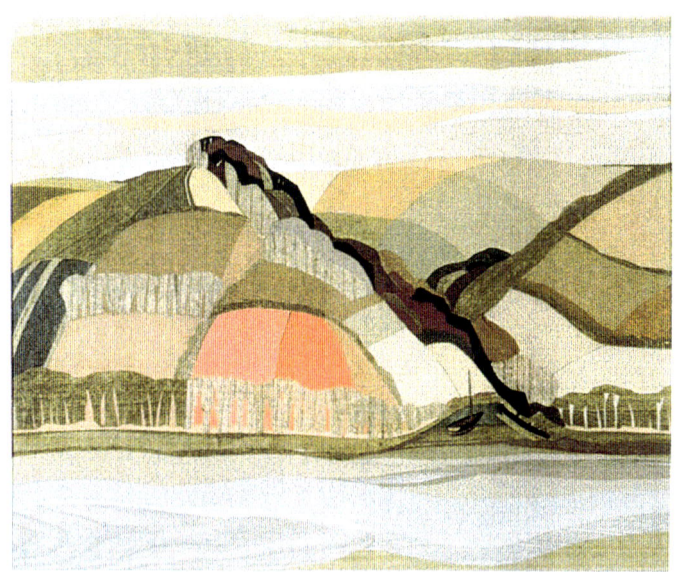

Another subject whose progress we can follow is the 'Old Slaughterhouse' and there are more examples available of this scene than almost any other.

Ruth must have made the initial charcoal drawing during the 1960's when they lived at Dartmouth,   The drawing is secure, and her interest in the intersection of vertical, horizontal and diagonal is evident.

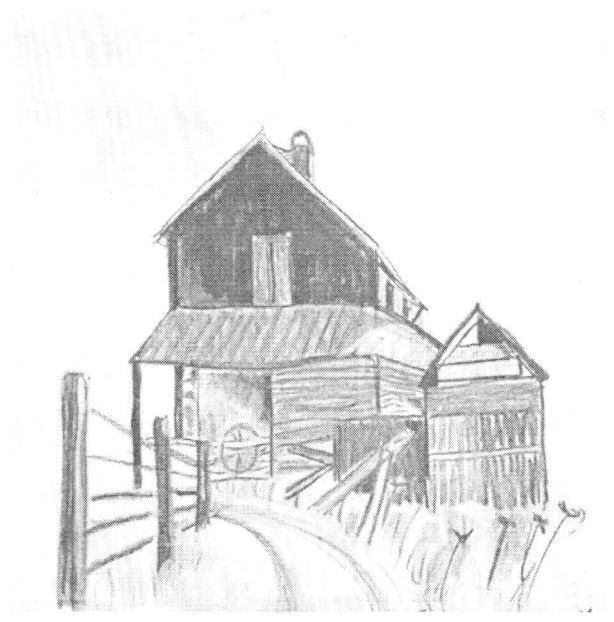

Plate 56, The Old Slaughterhouse, (Drawing) 13 x 14.

The oil painting (pl 57) was probably also done in the 1960's whereas the collage (58) was much later. In the collage we notice a shift in colour key from the oil where the ochres are more apparent than the dull earth reds, and relate more closely to the colours in the other sketch (59).

The proportions have also changed in the collage, with less foreground, as in pl 59, and more sky. The sky is created from a few simple shapes, and an element of warmth is achieved by making the foreground posts out of a rich mahogany-grained paper.

The stubble foreground is, appropriately enough, a paper composed of straw chips or some other plant material, and creates a textural foil to the plainer papers of the shed. Ruth has resisted the temptation to become drawn into *all* the surface textures of the subject, and wisely concentrated on just some of them.

There was also a less succesful watercolour, and a gouache from the side aspect of the building which I have included for the sake of interest (pl 60).

This concludes our look at works where the developmental process can be traced from first-hand study to final composition. Such transitions and transformations occur in the work of all artists, writers and composers, and the study of them greatly enhances our appreciation of the finished works.

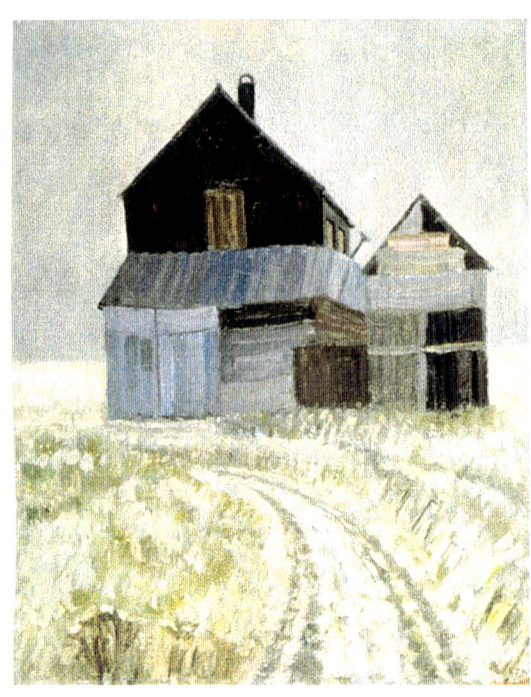

Plate 57.
Old Slaughterhouse,
Dartmouth,
(Oil)   20 x 16.

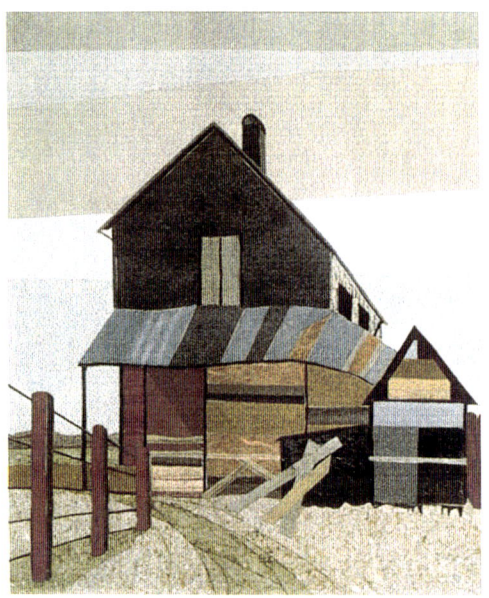

Plate 58.
Old Slaughterhouse,
Dartmouth,
(Collage)   13 x 11.

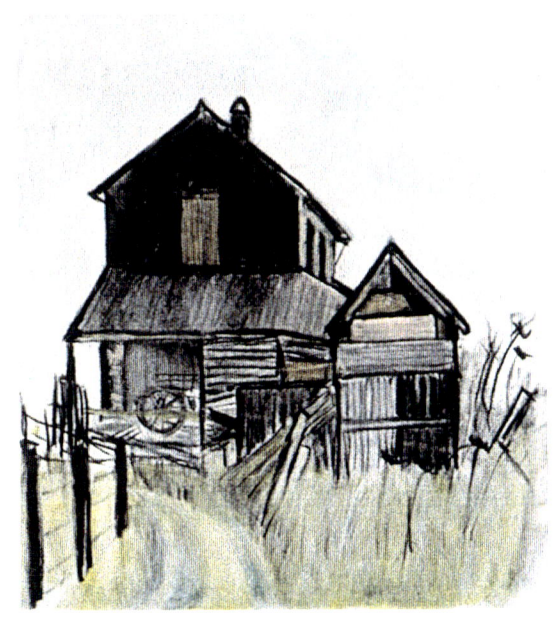

Plate 59. **Old Slaughterhouse,   (Charcoal & Wash)   15 x 13.**

Plate 60. **Old Slaughterhouse, (Gouache, black paper) 10 x 15.**

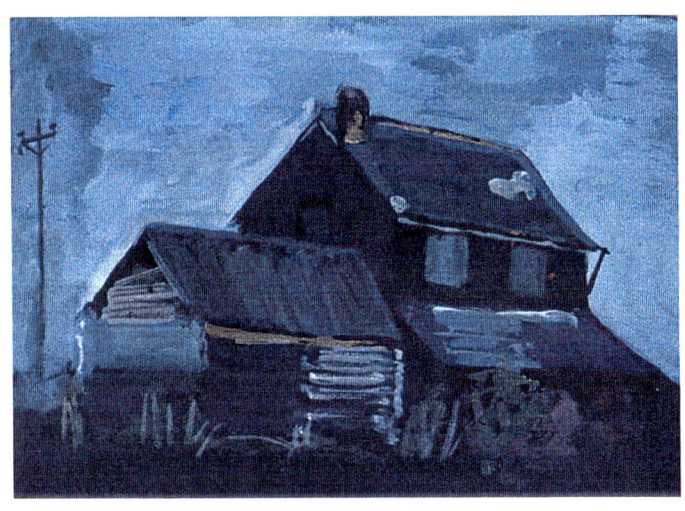

PART   THREE

LATER COLLAGES - SEA, COAST & ESTUARY.

In 1980 Ruth seems to have decided to concentrate on her real interests, and for the most part ceased to paint also for the summer visitors. Her sales book shows a marked decrease in numbers but an increase in her (extremely modest) prices.

In all the books Ruth possessed there seems to be no precedent for the way of working which she finally adopted. Nicholson and other artists also used cut papers in their reliefs, but I can find no evidence of anyone using the particular handmade papers she so enjoyed.

We must assume, then, that this arose naturally from her response to the actual material, and all that she had learnt from her studies of other artists was absorbed into the technique she subsequently evolved. With these works, which developed in the 1970's and came to fruition during the 80's, Ruth achieves her own synthesis of form and material.

Many of her collages of coastal scenes may be linked to oil paintings or drawings which she may still have had access to, but we will treat them here as 'fait accompli', except where certain influences spring to mind.

In 'The Cob, Lyme Regis' (pl 61) we do, for instance, notice a striking similarity between the building on the left and that in Reg Hayden's oil 'Poole Harbour' (see later), which has hung in her living room for as long as we can remember. The colour schemes are also very similar.

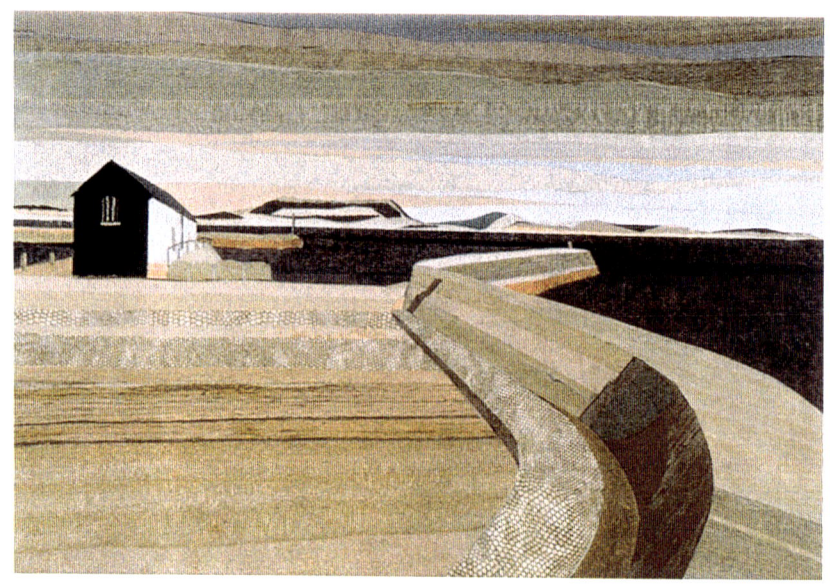

Plate 61.   The Cob, Lyme Regis (Collage) 11 x 16.

Plate 62.   Dungeness (Collage) 9 x 13.
Courtesy of Joy Brown.

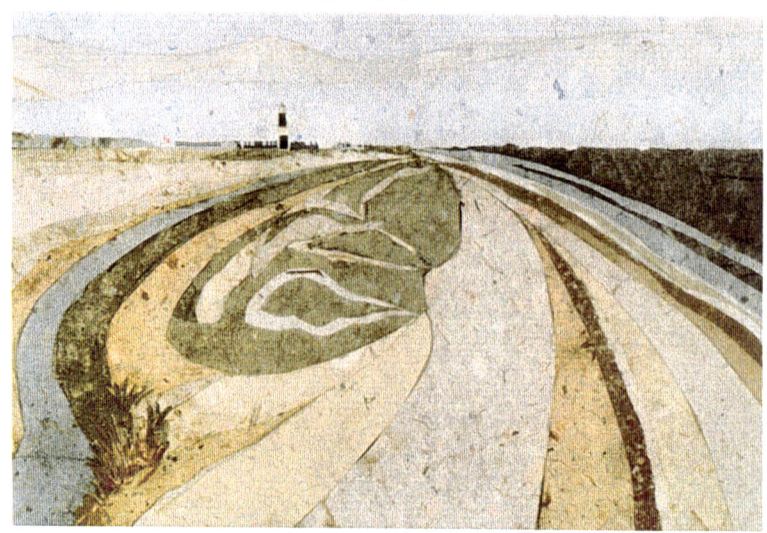

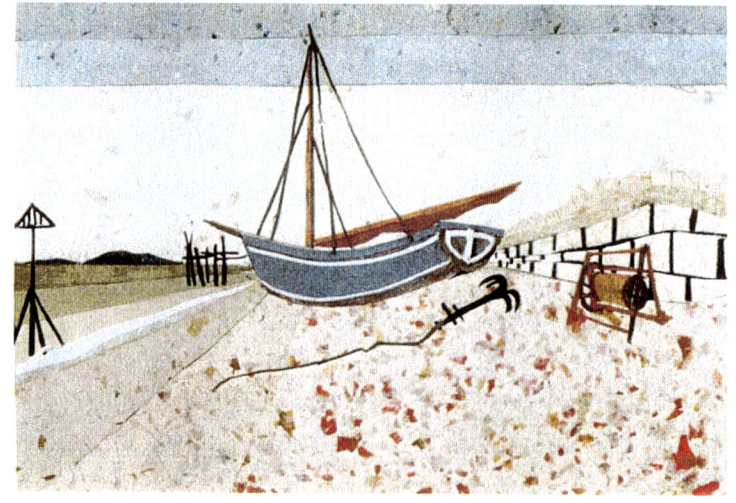

Plate 63.   Blue Boat (Collage)   6 x 8.

Plate 64.   Greek Harbour (Collage) 9 x 12.

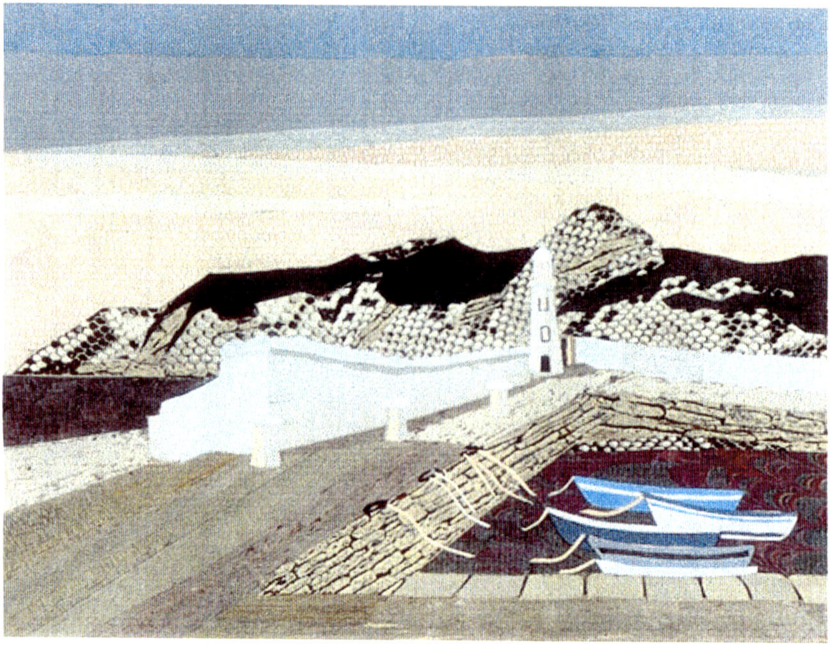

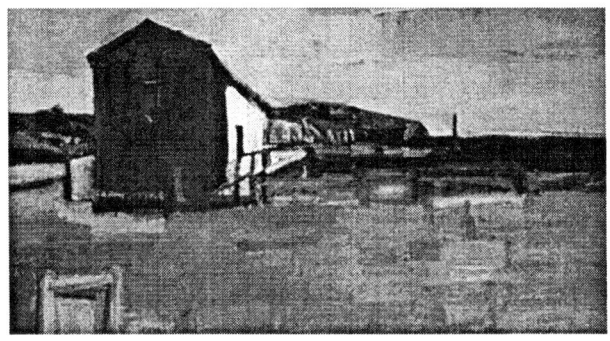

'Poole Harbour' by Reg Hayden (Oil).

In the collage (61) the building has been removed from the prominent position it enjoys in the oil above, and is recessed into the middle distance to allow it to be incorporated into a composition which includes the sweep of the Cob. This results in a slight discomfort between the perspectives of the Cob and building, which have not been entirely integrated.

'Dungeness' (plate 62) with its extraordinary bold sweep of foreground and tiny lighthouse (which is again placed almost exactly on the Golden section) is a rich and evocative work. The shapes in the middle distance are strangely evocative of pre-historic chalk figures such as the White Horse of Uffington; whereas in several of her collages it struck me, conversely, that the shapes of hills were somehow reminiscent of waves.

'Blue Boat' (pl 63), probably a late work, echoes Van Gogh's 'Boats on the beach at Saintes Maries de la Mer' with its delight in the elegant lines of the small craft. Ruth has also become involved with various artefacts on the beach, perhaps to some detriment of the overall composition. 'Greek Harbour' (pl 64) vividly evokes the southern sunshine, and the details of the mooring ropes are well integrated into the formal design.

'Cornish Harbour' (pl 65) is, to me, one of the most successful of these scenes. The complex shapes co-exist in elegant harmony, with the curve of the tideline creating a perfect foil for the verticals and horizontals of the quayside. It clearly owes something, consciously or unconsciously, to the St. Ives School painters - particularly Nicholson, Wallis and Scott - both in the simple colour chords and the naive shapes of the small boats.

'Happisburgh Lighthouse' (plate 66) has a crystalline quality which is almost impossible to reproduce adequately. Here, the exquisite detail is perfectly integrated into the whole composition, which in itself is so simple.

'Nash Point' (pl 67) is more complex in its construction, the sturdy shapes of the buildings caught between the gentle rhythms of sky and foreground. The gouache sketch of this scene (not shown), which was not considered by Ruth to be suitable for framing, is typically more simple and direct.

There are a number of beach and coastal scenes, and a few of the former are shown in the Conclusion as plates 80-82, while the latter will repay a more detailed examination.

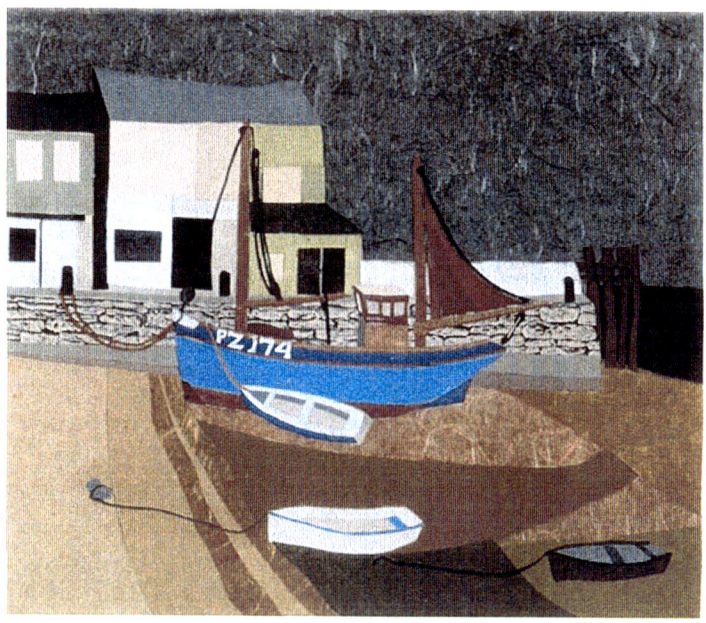

Plate 65.   Cornish Harbour & Fishing Boat (Collage),
            9 x 11.   *Courtesy of James & Wendy Gillett.*

Plate 66.   Happisburgh Lighthouse (Collage) 7 x 11.

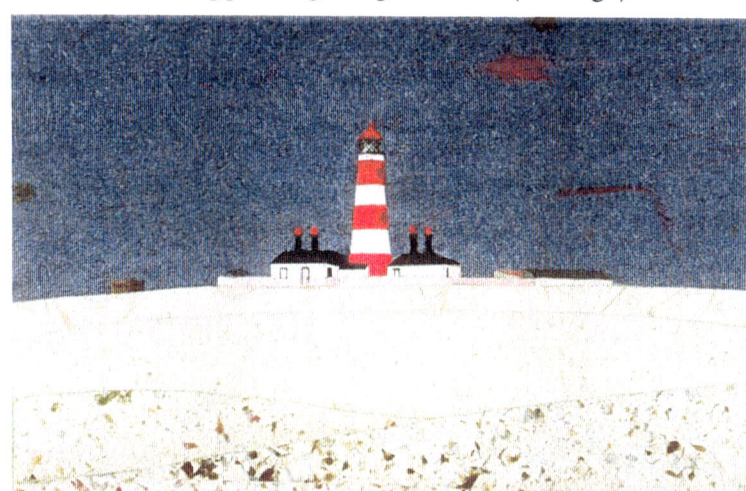

In the collages 'Carmarthen Bay, Low Tide', 'Sandscape [with setting sun]', and 'Estuary', (plates 68, 69 and 70 respectively) the metamorphosis of image into material is quite magical. The marbled papers *become* the pools and skyline, and our eyes are drawn and guided around the different shapes on the surface, and at the same time made aware of the illusion of depth and space. These pictures are to be looked *at* as well as looked through; the perpetual antithesis of the picture plane to the space it evokes is beautifully resolved.

Of these coastal scenes, 'Nolton Haven' (71) is the most serene. Ruth could not resist including the (real) boat winch in the foreground, but in this case it performs the vital role of anchoring the composition - cover it over and see how the whole picture would fall apart without it. The former views are almost agitated in their complex rhythms; greater stress on vertical & diagonal, together with a much wider colour scheme lead the eye in a lively dance which is indicative of the artist's ability to respond appropriately to a different motif. These rhythmic outlines created by the ebb and flow of tidal waters form the focus of attention in many of the later collages.

Not only does Ruth respond to a different subject by adjusting the formal means at her disposal, but aspects of the world that aroused her interest also found their form in an entirely different means of expression - the written word.

Her sentient response to the seashore in these collages is fully complemented by her gift for verbal expression. In her poem 'The Beach', (all these poems are quoted in full towards the end of this book) we see the .....

> "Porous, permeable, saturate ochre tract,
> Quicksanded quag, a sea-beleaguered land, ... "

In the same way that the visual material opens our mind by means of the eye, so her poetic images find their way into our imagination through her felicitous choice of words. These lines, with their delicate consonontal chimes are, consciously or not, set in the tradition of Welsh poesy, whereby the sound of the words is regarded as having equal parity with its sense.

Anyone familiar with Welsh language poetry will be fully aware of this, but it can also be appreciated through the English language writings of Gerard Manley Hopkins (from whom I borrow the phrase 'consonontal chimes') and Dylan Thomas.

Ruth's poem 'Summer Afternoon' shows a sensitivity to the peacefulness of the landscape equal to that displayed in 'The Beach'.

> "The suffocating stillness fills all space
> suspending life within the quivering air."

120

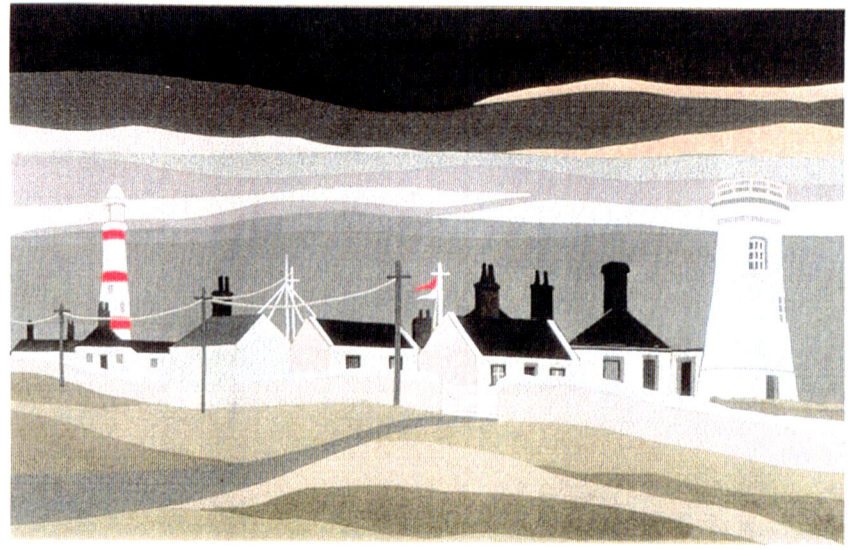

Plate 67.   Nash Point, St. Donats, Glamorgan   (Collage),
11 x 18.   *Courtesy of Dr & Mrs G.E. Phillips.*

Plate 68.   Carmarthen Bay, Low Tide (Collage) 13 x 22.

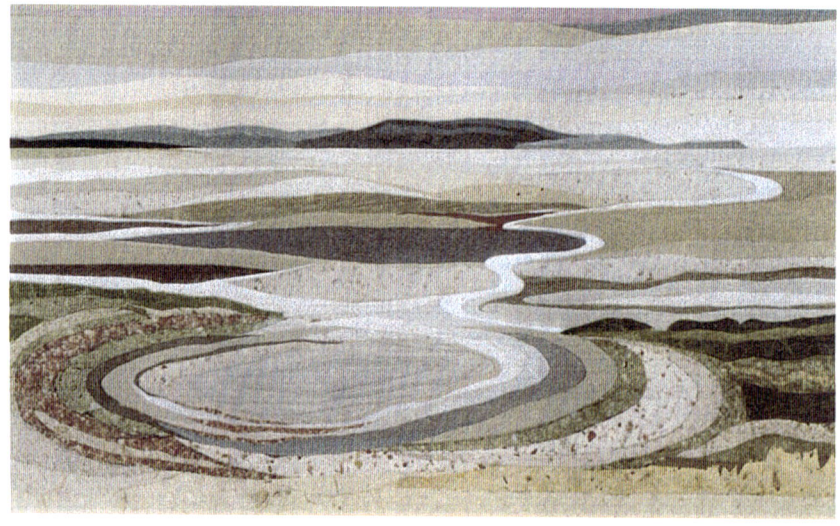

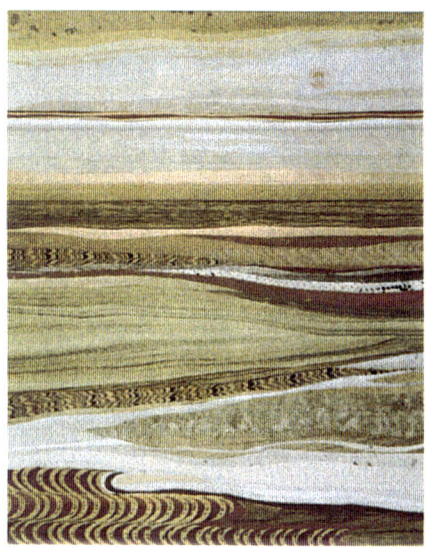 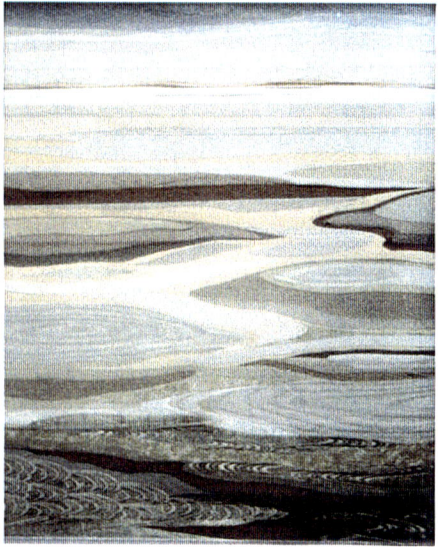

Plate 69. Sandscape (Collage).   Plate 70. Estuary (Collage).

Plate 71.   Nolton Haven, Pembrokeshire (Collage).

Pls 70 & 71 courtesy of Mr & Mrs C.W. Isherwood.

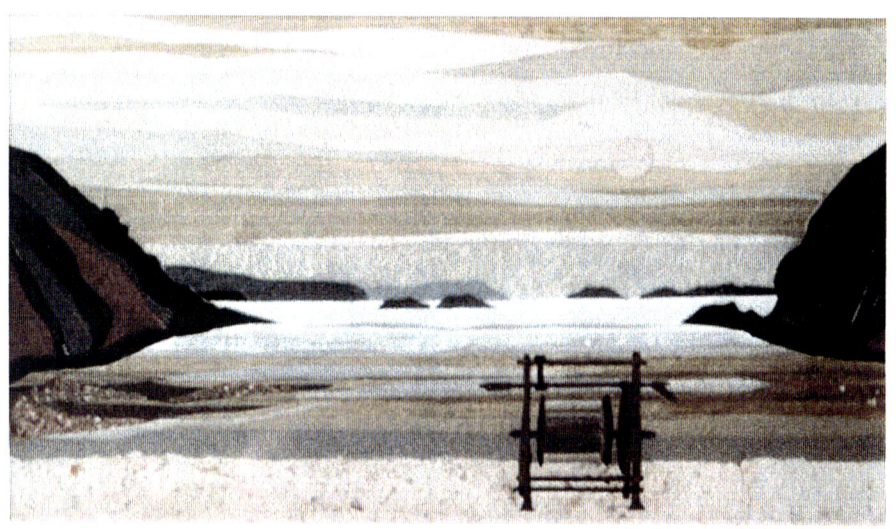

Then, in 'Snow II' we are invited .....

"To look again with a cured perception
At a world miraculously transformed."

Snow certainly transforms the world, but the world is also transformed by our perception of it, and that perception in turn is informed by works of art and poetry. Contemporary arts unfreeze our concepts of what we thought things were like, and our changing views of 'reality' are determined as much by the vision of the poet as by that of the physicist.

Ruth's poem 'Modern Art', however, clearly indicates a lack of sympathy with 20th Century painting :-

"The Impressionists I view with pleasure
The sun, the light in liberal measure:
But when it comes to Modern Art
The abstract plays too large a part."

and .....

"I'll go once more with open mind,
All prejudice I'll put behind
To look at works by such as Klee,
Picasso, Braque, Matisse, Dufy."

and finally .....

"Cubists and Surrealists have their fashion
But they provoke me to an angry passion,
And so I turn in unrepentant flight
To the sad smile of a Pre-Raphaelite."

One wonders to what extent it is entirely serious when so much of her work *does* betray a certain affinity with, say, the Cubists - although not with the Surrealists.   Perhaps this poem was written in the late 1950's or early 1960's before Ruth had begun to get to grips with this kind of work. Also, in a curious way, an outright statement of criticism or disagreement sometimes causes the subconscious mind to set up a compensating movement in the other direction.

Her mature works are never as challenging as ..... "Picasso, Braque, Matisse, Dufy", but neither are they to be compared with the "sad smile of a Pre-Raphaelite". However, I suggest that whatever she felt at the time of writing this poem, she did indeed " ...... go once more with open mind" and the effects of this unprejudicial attitude were far-reaching.

We will end our appreciation of Ruth's late collages with two lovely works expressing her response to the landscape.

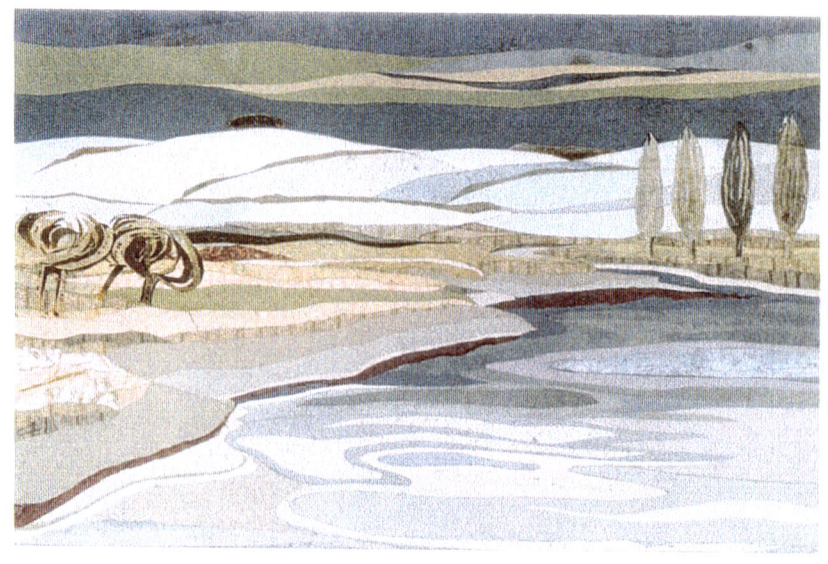

Plate 72.   Thames at Wallingford, under Snow (Collage) 11 x 17.
Plate 73.   Holts, near Avebury (Collage) 13 x 13.

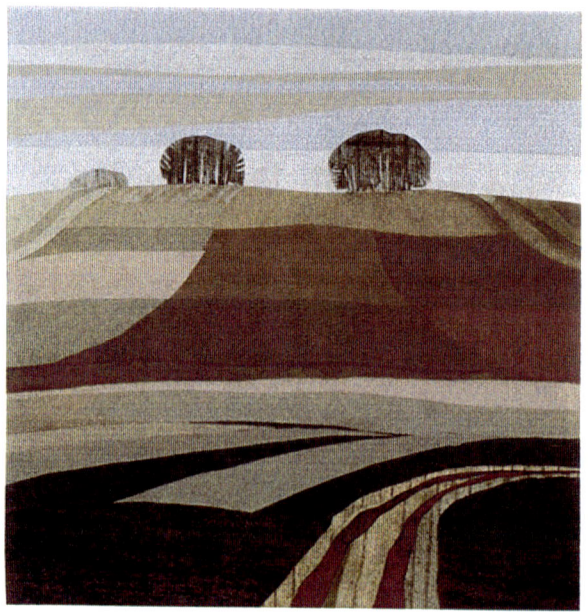

The colours in 'Thames at Wallingford under Snow' (pl 72) are at once perfectly evocative of such a scene and, in the abstract sense, perfectly in tune - being built around the complementary chord of yellow ochre and indigo, with a dash of aquamarine to complete the harmony. This work does not quite achieve the simplicity of design shown in the next painting, but is nevertheless full of rhythmic interest.

'Holts, near Avebury' (plate 73) has a more limited palette (though still difficult to reproduce !), based on the central rich brown, with the other shades veering subtly towards madder, indigo and lime green.

Its strength also lies in a taut geometrical construction: The simple sweep of the field edges culminates in the two clumps of trees, and the lower horizontal line above the foreground curve lies, again, on the golden section - thereby giving a firm base to the two (almost) parabolic [1] curves which are the edges of the fields leading up to the clumps.

The two field edges are in fact only halves of the full curves (the mirror image of each would be outside the picture area), nevertheless they carry the eye in a satisfying sweep up to the horizon, culminating in the two clumps of trees.

1.   A parabola is a symmetrical curve which moves around a point, or focus, upon a fixed axis in such a way that its distance from the point, and between a fixed line which underlies it, always remain in constant ratio.   It is one of the conic sections (together with the circle, ellipse and hyperbola) which were first defined by Greek mathematicians. These geometrical curves, because of their inherent rationality, lend coherence to any design whether abstract or figurative.

These pictures, together with the few other plates not described in detail, show us an artist always pressing towards her limits. Some are less successful than others; well, "even Homer nodded" as the old saying goes, and in the context of an artist's whole output, even the minor errors of judgement or execution are curiously endearing.

We may conclude by reminding ourselves of the three precepts of the Bauhaus, briefly outlined in Part One, and the extent to which they can be identified in Ruth's work. Firstly, she extracted from her material - the handmade papers - a unique expressive potential which seems to owe nothing directly to other works she had seen.

Secondly she possessed a natural sense of design, and although this was undoubtedly sharpened by the exercises done at art school, I would hazard a guess that the many instances of formal sophistication in her work were intuitive rather than conscious.

Thirdly, her library shows that the analysis and appreciation of a wide spectrum of art forms was part of her everyday experience, whether for their 'structural properties' or enjoyed for other reasons. Thus, without attending any full time training, we can see that of her own volition she assimilated all the factors which the Bauhaus teachers laid down as constituting a sound education in the visual arts.

130

Plate 74.
Archways,
perspective,
(Watercolour)
   14 x 10.

Plate 75.
Woodland Rides,
Autumn (Collage),
   11 x 18.

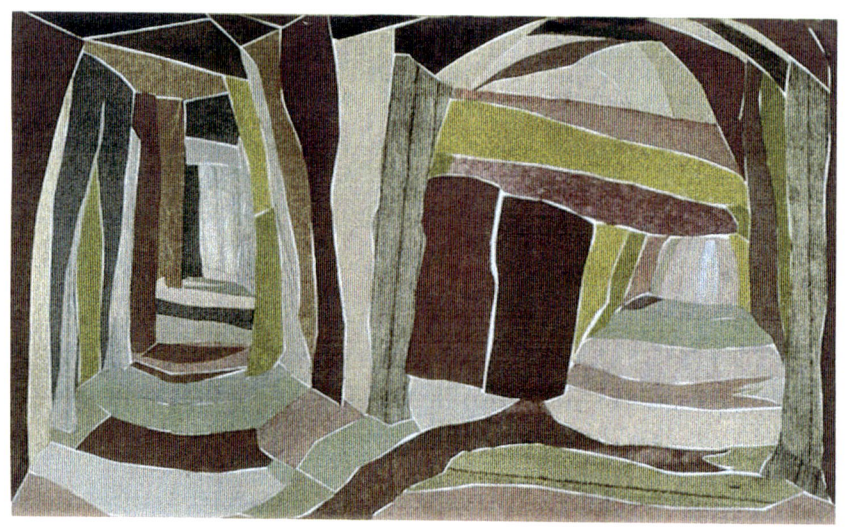

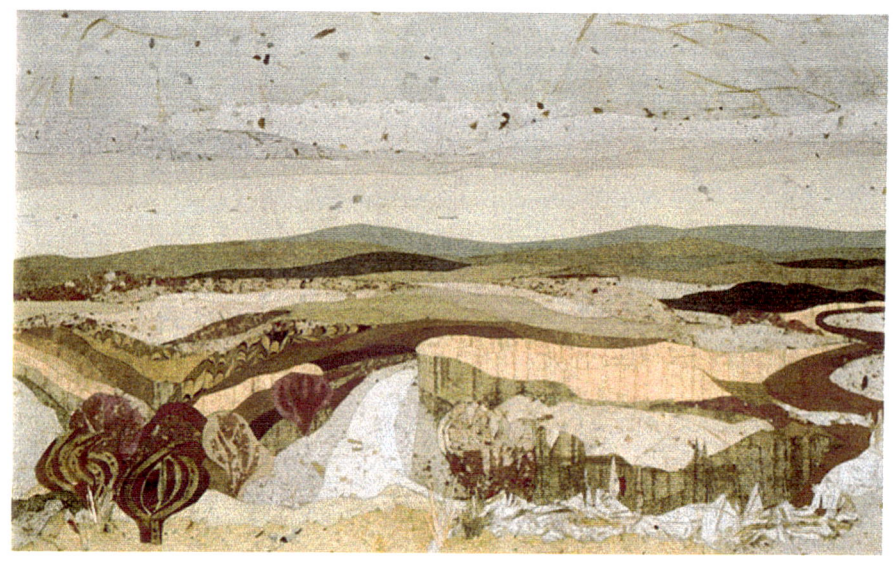

Plate 76.   Romney Marsh   (Collage) 11 x 18.
Plate 77.   Ridgeway at Uffington (Collage) 15 x 23.

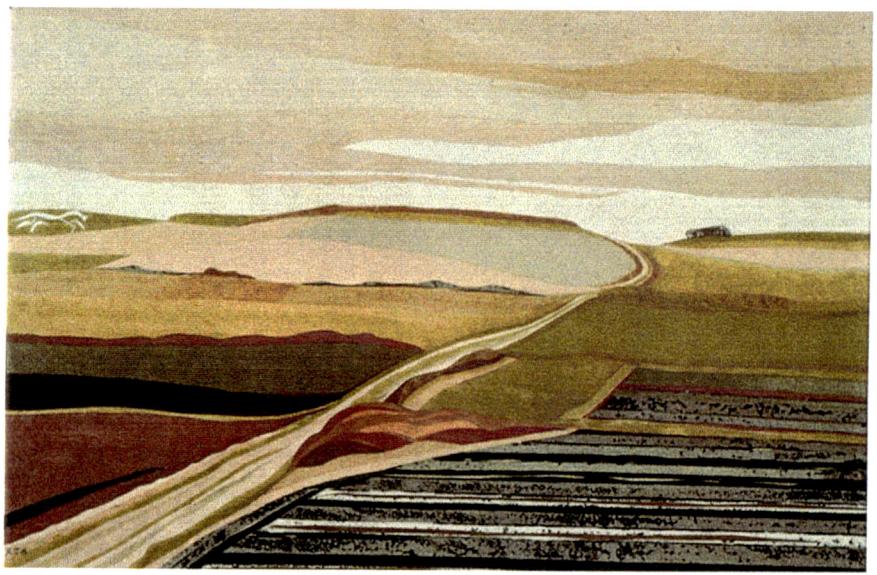

CONCLUSION

In this volume we have looked at the many influences which contributed to the shaping of Ruth's identity as an artist, and the particular pictures reproduced have been those relevant to the influences considered in the greatest depth. However, she had many other interests, as her books and cuttings show, which are not directly applicable to this selection.

We are all stimulated not only by those who see the world as we do, but by those who see it quite differently, and her very broad selection of reference material bears witness to her open-mindedness. This attitude extended to poetry, literature, musical criticism and philosophy, and her own poems show that she had a real gift for verbal expression. The fact that these poems only came to light after her death indicates a (surely) unwarranted modesty in this respect.

Had she had the benefit of discussion with other writers, and their critical approbation, one wonders whether she would have been encouraged, and allowed herself to pursue this creative vein further. She had listed, in addition to those poems which materialised (see Vol I), many other subjects about which she wished to write, such as :-

Lighthouses, Windmill, Autumn bonfire, Locks, Buoys, Child posting letter, Golgotha, White road over hills at night, Noah's Ark, A bath, Lamplighter, Contrariness, The old car, Choirboys, Willows, Falling tree, Chess, Horseshoe, Waves, Hour-glass, Thankfulness, Conventional lying versus truth, Washing on the line, 7's, Coal, Weir, ... and many more.

It was interesting to compare this list with that of her 'Painting subjects' (both lists dating from the 1950's), and to see that 'Washing on the line, Golgotha and Road over hills at night' appear in both.

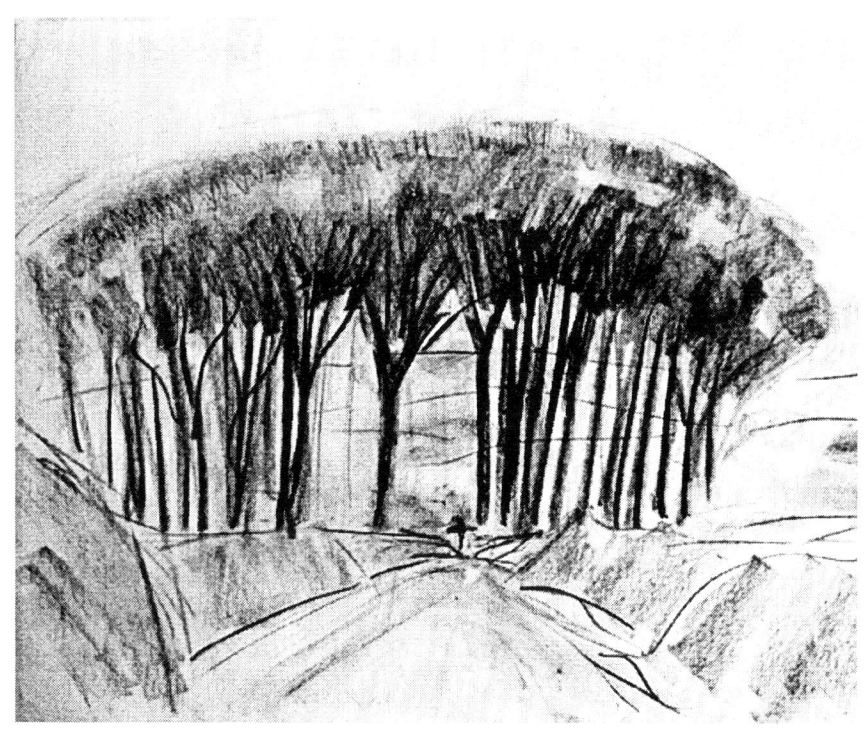

Plate 78.   Over hill into wood (Drawing) 14 x 19.

Ruth had collected folders full of quotations or the whole poems of others, not just cuttings but often retyped or handwritten. Many of them (infuriatingly) do not quote the exact source of the item in question, but then she was not primarily an academic.

Nevertheless we can glean from them the kind of subjects and views which interested her. Certain names reappear regularly: 20th Century poets include Winifred Holtby, Alfred Noyes (as well as his poems there was a short extract entitled 'Arguments for a First Cause'), Edwin Muir, Robert Frost, Dylan Thomas, and very many lesser known names.

The contents of her Art cuttings folder are eclectic in the extreme, including an article on 'The Uncertainty Principle in Art' by Alan Davie, and 'Figurative Art as a New Abstraction', as well as many closely typed pages on individual artists and various schools of painting. Extracts dating from 1960 indicate an interest in Carl Jung, and articles by Arthur Koestler also crop up several times.

Ruth listened avidly to classical music and also subscribed for some time to The Listener which, in those days, contained much food for thought. She had many cuttings about new recordings and reviews of concerts, and had also taped innumerable Radio 3 programmes.

She was very organised both in work and domesticity, with a flair for interior design as the colour scheme in the living-room of their cottage shows - a lovely combination of dull blues and old gold, complemented by the colours of the prints and paintings she and Michael bought.

These comprised, amongst others, the fine oil painting by Reg Hayden of the 'Harbour Entrance, Poole' shown earlier, 'Nature Morte' by the French artist Lucien Mainsseux, and signed lithographs of harbour scenes by William Scott (1951) and Keith Vaughan (1953). There was also the lithograph 'Lighthouse' by de Staël, a powerful chalk drawing by Ray Howard Jones entitled 'Ghosts of Abereiddy', an atmospheric oil of Caldy Island by Rick Bradforth, and an H.M. Bateman cartoon 'The Critic' - with its original copperplate woodblock.

The de Staël litho hung boldly in the kitchen, while the predominantly blues, yellows and blacks of the other works enhanced the colours of the living-room - which also featured a profusion of decorative chinaware, pottery and glass 'objets', and antique furniture, all collected patiently at modest cost over a long period by her and Michael.

Incidentally, Ruth's consciousness of the need to match colours was particularly acute with regard to the mounts and frames for her own pictures, where she was very particular about what would 'go'.

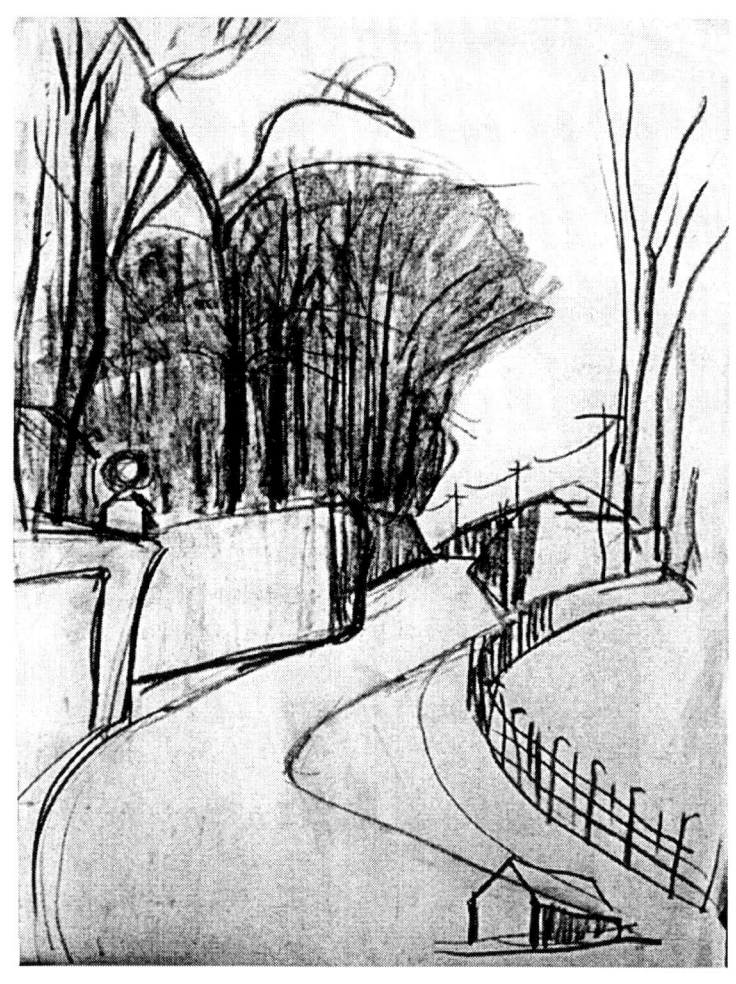

Plate 79.   Road past wood   (Drawing)   18 x 14.

Despite her warm outgoing personality - and one remembers also a deliciously wry sense of humour - Ruth was also a very private and independent person, and this may in part have militated against her seeking, generally, to be a part of a group of artists. She did, though, get much practical support and encouragement from Michael - particularly after they retired and he was no longer periodically away at sea.

But above these other qualities, it is her kindness, bravery and generosity which linger in the memory. One would never have guessed that she was in almost constant pain, and I can remember her amused remark regarding Michael's limp (as a result of polio), "we've only got one good leg between us".

Amongst the poetry cuttings was a note of a comment by, probably, Winifred Holtby - "What do you do when you find you're living inside a bad joke ?", which evidently paralleled Ruth's own situation. Her uncomplaining ability to create humour out of extreme discomfort was part of her nature which sought - and therefore found - the best in others, a trait to which her many friends will bear witness.

As an artist we have seen how 'all that she had met' became a part of her work, and after experimenting with many different subjects and materials she gradually narrowed her range down to the collages which formed the bulk of her output during the last few years of her life. She was at once very self-critical but also very determined with regard to her work, and was still working, albeit very slowly, two months before she died.

Late collages such as the pair of beach scenes 'Paddlers' and 'Edwardian holidaymakers' (81, 82), and 'Millmead Lock' (84) are remarkable enough, but the intensity of her struggle in the last few years is really echoed in the gem-like quality of works such as 'Edwardian Beach scene' and 'Thames Barge' (80 & 83), and of course in the collage 'Quintet' shown earlier as plate 18.

In these she seems to have truly achieved in her chosen material a synthesis between her early interests in abstract form and an ongoing fascination with the details of life, the way things are made and how they reveal their construction to the observant eye.

We can only be glad of an artist such as Ruth who, by pursuing the materialisation of her vision without compromise, and to the best of her ability, allows us to .....

> "Look again with a cured perception
> At a world miraculously transformed".

*   *   *   *   *   *   *

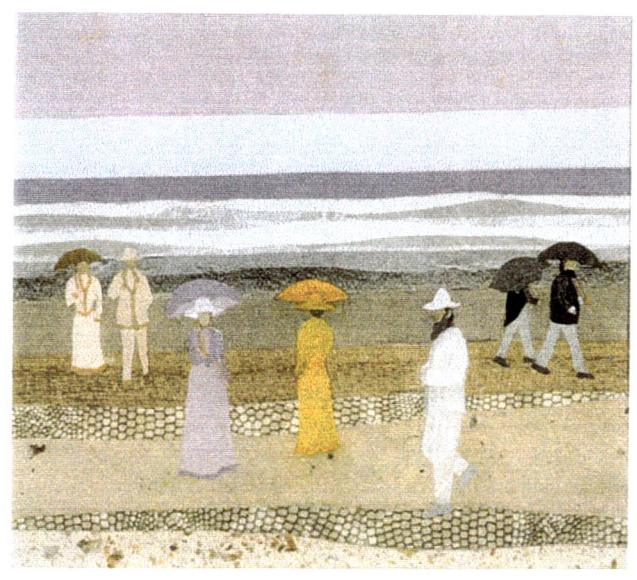

Plate 80.   Edwardian Beach Scene (Collage) 7 x 8.

Plate 81.   Paddlers (Collage),
9 x 7.   *Courtesy of Joice Acton.*

Plate 82.   Edwardian Holidaymakers (Collage) 10 x 7.

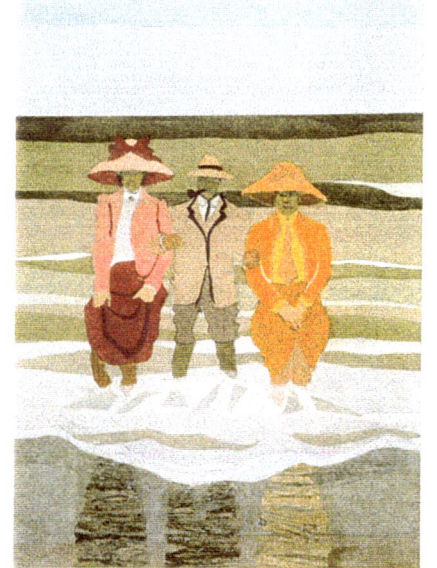

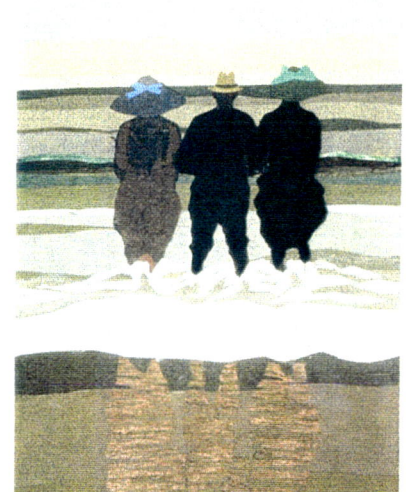

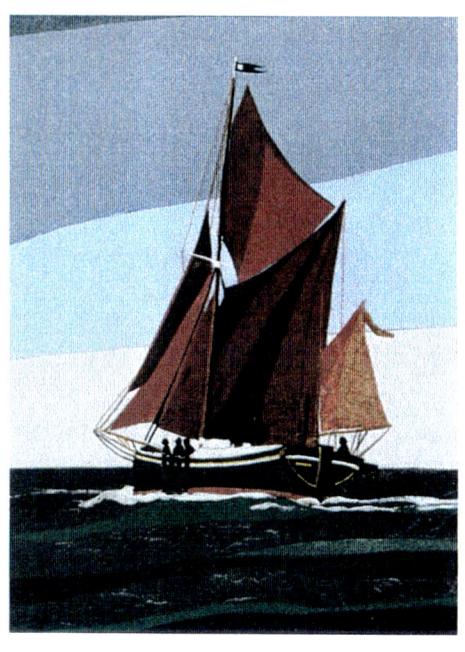

Plate 83.
Thames Barge,
(Collage) 8 x 6.

*Plates 82 & 83 courtesy of
Mr & Mrs R.I. Stansbury.*

Plate 84.
Millmead Lock,
Wey Navigation,
near Guildford,
(Collage) 17 x 20.

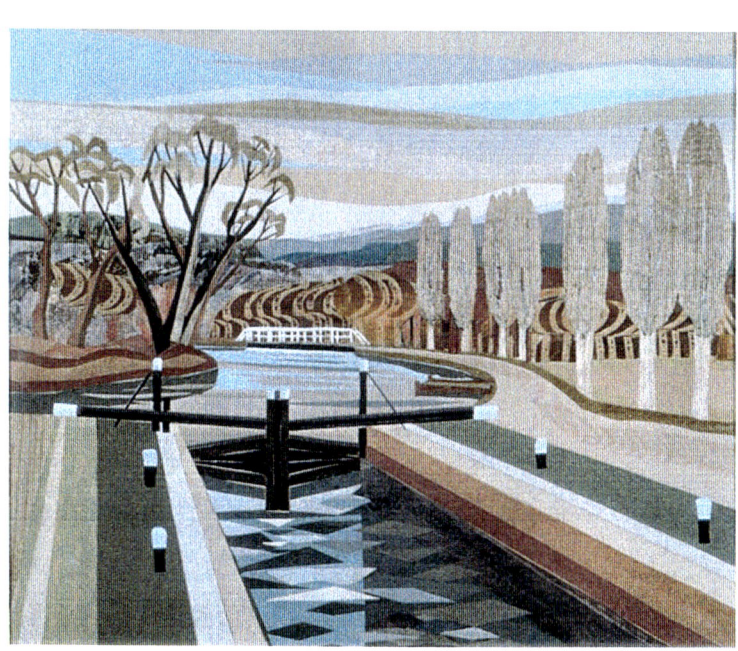

APPENDIX

(Poems referred to in the main body of the text).

The Beach.

Infinitesimal grains of limitless sand,
Palate-ridged dunes of myriad-particled shore,
Printless, obliterate, wind-whipped infinite strand
Eternally sun-warmed, moon-bleached desert floor.

Octopus seaweed, tentacle-torn till beached,
Porpoised planks flung free by wave washed power,
Dolphin-dipped, till seventh wave o'erreached
When moon recalled the ocean from its scour.

Porous, permeable, saturate ochre tract,
Quicksanded quag, a sea-beleaguered land,
Exposed, erased, by shorebound rollers racked,
Reclaimed, soon lost to the same relentless hand.

Snow II.

Snow, snow flying, spinning joyfully,

Floating and sailing over the world:

White of the whitest peerless beauty

Loosed from the overweighted cloud.

More on more and for ever gently

Piling and banking, smoothing the angles

Of man's red brick imperfections

Falls the immaculate sinless shroud.

Surely a sign inescapable

To silenced Wellington-booted man

To look again with a cured perception

At a world miraculously transformed.

Modern Art.

The Impressionists I view with pleasure
The sun, the light in liberal measure:
But when it comes to Modern Art
The abstract plays too large a part.

I'll go once more with open mind,
All prejudice I'll put behind
To look at works by such as Klee,
Picasso, Braque, Matisse, Dufy.

Straight in its eye I look the first,
Determined I shall know the worst,
But when I try my gaze to free
The eye stares balefully back at me.

Next on the line - a hard blue sky,
A torso with a skull nearby:
A squashèd watch, a bleachèd strand,
A strange abominable land.

The third I see is labelled "nude",
Without a doubt her health is rude,
The flesh looks overripe, contused,
One wonders if she's been misused.

Cubists and Surrealists have their fashion,
But they provoke me to an angry passion,
And so I turn in unrepentant flight
To the sad smile of a Pre-Raphaelite.

Heredity.

The faces of one's fellow men
Cause one to pause - to pause and question
What in their mould conspires to lend
Such diversity of expression.

The droop of mouth in characteristic pose
Points the prevailing mood: But can a chin
Indicate temperament ?   Of what account
That strange elusive likeness to one's kin ?

Mendel unlocked the vast genetic plan
Of chromosomes in complex variance.
But what looks out of the eyes of every man
Is human love, or hate, or plain indifference.

Summer Afternoon.

An interval of cumulating silence falls
Upon the post-noon limbo of the day:
Even the ineffectual hot-breath breeze
Dies in the face of a heat which grows apace
Until, tiptoed, one strains all ears to hear
A stray leaf turn within the motionless trees,
A feather lift, a twig snap underfoot;
The suffocating stillness fills all space
Suspending life within the quivering air.

A shrinking board inside the empty house
Protests;   only the slanting shafts of light
Reveal the specks of dust in downward drift.

A bumble-bee benignly on his way
Zooms against a pane - and time released
Resumes its rare-disputed sway.

Acknowledgements

We have been able to produce this book with substantially less consultation than was appropriate for Volume I, but in particular would like to thank Wendy Gillett for kindly agreeing to write the Preface. For proof-reading and suggestions for the text we thank Liz Hurton and Beryl John, and Linda Harvey (a.k.a. 'Heliotrope Publishing') has done a sterling job of the practical publishing.

Once again we are grateful to all those friends and relatives who kindly allowed their pictures to be photographed, and for their consents to print them. A number of additional paintings have come to light since Vol I was produced (and it is hoped that more will continue to do so). We have been able to use some of these and others have been earmarked for Vol III.

John Hunter has excelled again, this time in reprocessing Ruth's old Instamatic photographs so that we could make use of some important pictures not otherwise available to us. To the unknown owners of those pictures we extend our thanks in anticipation of ever meeting them, and hope that not too much detail or colour fidelity has been lost along the way.

Elizabeth Haines.

David Harvey.

INDEX *(excluding 'Plates')*